UNTETHER

UNTETHER

Inspiration for Living Free and Strong
No Matter What the Challenge

By JT Mestdagh

Foreword by Dr. Nido R. Qubein

Praise for UNTETHER

In an era of "victim chic," JT's story is a refreshing reminder that while we don't choose our circumstances, we do choose our response. JT's determination to respond to life's challenges with love, faith and joy is an inspiring model for us all.

— LYNN VINCENT

New York Times bestselling co-author, Heaven is for Real and Same Kind of Different as Me

JT is the most extraordinary student I have worked with in my 45 years of teaching reading. His incredible resilience and persistence, in spite of life-threatening medical disabilities, as well as dyslexia are an inspiration and challenge to us all. UNTETHER will leave you crying on one page and cheering on another. I recommend this book for parents of struggling students, as well as young adults who feel overwhelmed by their difficulties in life.

— STEPHAN TATTUM, M.A.

Program Director, LearnUP Reading Clinic. Reading & Math Specialist at Sterne School, San Francisco. Program Director of Denver Academy from 1973-2008

I stand in awe of JT's honesty and determination as he shares experiences from his journey to wellness, so that others can be better prepared for their own journey. In UNTETHER, he recounts through his pure and raw emotions, how he endured all that his medical condition and the numerous healthcare providers put his body and mind through. He shares how he found the strength to overcome these challenges in the unconditional love of his parents, the rock-solid foundation of his faith and the courage in his heart.

— PRAMOD P. REDDY, MD

Division Director, Division of Pediatric Urology. Professor of Surgery. Cincinnati Children's Hospital Medical Center

UNTETHER made me laugh, cry, crave justice and desire fairness for everyone who find themselves in similar circumstances. It also built my faith to see God's comforting hand holding on tight in the turbulence. If you are a mom, dad, grandma or grandpa, or anyone who cares about kids—you will love this story.

— EMILIE P. WIERDA
Educational Advocate

UNTETHER is a celebration of faith. Every single adverse event and obstacle that JT and his parents found in their long journey, were confronted with faith, and the result was always something positive. In every episode of this wonderful story, the characteristic sincere, fresh and powerful eternal smile of JT emerges triumphant.

One of the main lessons learned from the reading of UNTETHER is that every problem that we human beings confront, represents an opportunity to create something good. Not all patients and families are strong enough to overcome those multiple challenges. JT's parents deserve my admiration and respect for all what they went through, as well as the love, unconditional support and care provided to JT. The entire family came out victorious after the odyssey and in addition they found in JT's life a meaning. The birth of JT turned into an inspiration. JT is here for a reason.

— ALBERTO PEÑA, MD, FAAP, FACS, FRCS
Ponzio Family Chair for Colorectal Pediatric Surgery. Director, International Center for Colorectal Care. Children's Hospital Colorado. Professor of Surgery University of Colorado. Anschutz Medical Campus, Aurora, Colorado

Publisher:
Elite Online Publishing
63 E 11400 S #230
Sandy, UT 84070
EliteOnlinePublishing.com

ISBN: 978-1513649993

This book is set in Dyslexie font. (The eBook version may appear different depending upon the device.) This unique typeface is designed for people with dyslexia to make reading, learning, and working easier — and more fun. (It helped me get through school! — JTM)
Learn more at Dyslexiefont.com

To learn more and to receive updates visit
JTMestdagh.com/book

DEDICATION

To My Parents

Throughout writing this book I learned so much about myself. But the most amazing part was discovering all that you did for me growing up. I have always thought being the patient is the easy part and being the caretaker is the most difficult. I have found this to be so true after learning what you had to go through.

I am so thankful for the amazing decisions you made for me, the strength you developed in times of uncertainty and frustration, as well as the faith you shared with me and the parents, kids, medical people, and teachers who were part of our journey.

Mom, thank you for praying every night with me and for finding so many resources that supported me! Dad, thank you for always being the kind, strong hand even in the toughest situations and for being my coach through all things. You two made our family strong. You're the reason for my success. I love you.

TABLE OF CONTENTS

FOREWORD

I am inspired by the life of JT Mestdagh.
From childhood to now, JT has demonstrated faithful
courage and true grit.
By all accounts, he could have gotten discouraged and
given up.
But, not JT.

He believes that God has a plan for his life. And he
moves onward with forward thinking.
He believes in the art of the possible.
He believes there is no such thing as "unrealistic
dreams." Only "unrealistic timelines."

He is blessed with parents who love him.
And mentors who guide him.
He is a role model for all of us: When things get tough,
the tough must get going!

You'll love this book.
It is the story of a remarkable young man.
His fears. His pursuits. His accomplishments.
His story will encourage you.

I've known JT for almost six years now. Ever since he visited High Point University in High Point, North Carolina.

He impressed me when I first met him.

And he went on to be actively involved in campus life, leading along the way with ethics and extraordinary manners.

It was evident JT would be a leader. An innovator. A positive thinker.

JT wrote this book to inform, persuade, and motivate others.

Life can be difficult—but it isn't impossible.

As you read this book, you'll find yourself crying and laughing.

It's a good book.

And you'll want to share it with others.

—*Nido R. Qubein*
President
High Point University
High Point, North Carolina

PROLOGUE
Why I Created This Book

Are you someone with medical or physical challenges? So am I.

Do you learn differently than the majority of people? Think differently? Me too.

Are you a parent or family member or friend of somebody like that? My family and friends know all about living with and helping someone who's different—someone who has to navigate the world every day using special tools, techniques, and tricks to cope and achieve; someone who has to be positive and patient and persistent, even when they don't feel like it.

You're why I spent two years pulling this book together.

It was a lot of hard work, but it will be worth it if it encourages you and helps you to *never give up.*

This book is my story, but maybe it tells some of your story too. I hope you'll feel less alone and more confident. I hope you'll "untether" yourself from fears and limiting beliefs. I hope it will build your faith in yourself and in God. And I hope you'll share it with others. Together we can show the world we're overcomers!

— *JT Mestdagh*
Grosse Pointe, Michigan

Chapter 1

#MIRACLE

When something bad happens you have three choices. You can let it define you, you can let it destroy you, or you can let it strengthen you.

— Dr. Seuss

The morning after I was born, a very large stranger walked into my mom's hospital room. The sun was barely up, the shades were still down, and Mom was only half awake.

"Mrs. Mestdagh, my name is Dr. Fredrick Rector," said the man. "I'm a pediatric surgeon. I need you to sign these papers so that I can operate on your son today." He lifted the clipboard he was holding.

My mom blinked in the dim light. She had a really awful headache and felt groggy, but she tried to focus on the tall doctor standing over her. She was sure he was wrong. She had seen me when I was born the night before, and I looked perfect.

"There must be some mistake, doctor," she whispered. She took a deep breath and her voice got stronger. "Maybe you're in the wrong room."

"No, I'm afraid not, Mrs. Mestdagh," said the surgeon. His voice boomed. "You gave birth to a boy last night, did you not? Unfortunately, your son was born with TEF—tracheoesophageal fistula—as well as esophageal atresia and a high imperforated anus. We must operate on him today, or he will —"

"Wait!"

My father walked into the room.

"She doesn't know!"

● ● ●

My mom and dad—their names are Kristine (Kris) Boll and James (Jim) Mestdagh—had been excited about becoming parents. They had been married for four years and were full of love and faith and optimism. Mom's pregnancy had gone well. Then I decided to come three weeks early.

Looking back, Mom remembers that her *Daily Bread* devotional reading for September 13, 1995, was on trusting God and depending upon the power of prayer. She didn't know it at the time, but she and Dad were going to learn a lot about prayer—the hard way.

Mom's water broke at 3:20 a.m. Neither of them could go back to sleep, so Dad did some laundry, packed Mom's suitcase, and vacuumed the house. We laugh about that now. He likes things clean and orderly. The family teases him by calling him anal, which was ironic, given what we were about to face.

They called the obstetrician, Dr. Zalenski. He said to get to the hospital right away.

They reached St. John Hospital & Medical Center in Detroit, Michigan, around 7 a.m. It's a few miles from our home in Grosse Pointe Shores. When Mom was finally given an epidural at around 5:30 p.m. they accidently nicked her spinal column. That would be the cause of some terrible headaches for the next week. Poor Mom. But other than that, the labor went fine.

Except not everything was fine. My parents didn't realize that having a dozen specialists in the birthing room was unusual. I was having a hard time arriving. When I came at 8:07 p.m., weighing 5 pounds 2 ounces, I looked blue. Dad "cut the cord." Then the nurses rushed me to the "nursery"—which actually was the Neonatal Intensive Care Unit (NICU). My parents wouldn't be able to hold me for a week.

Dad and Mom called family and friends to announce my arrival. After a little while, Dad told Mom he was going home for the night. Mom was a bit disappointed about that, but she was exhausted and knew he was tired too. She was just very happy that the ordeal was over.

Well, it had just begun, actually. And Dad didn't go straight home. He first went to the NICU to talk to the doctors. What was going on with his son?

● ● ●

The night was dark when Dad finally drove home along Lake Shore Drive. He hadn't gone through labor, but he was beat. And sad and worried.

Dad walked into the empty house and switched on a light. Our dog Kody jumped joyfully all over him, but Dad wasn't in the mood to play. He barely had the strength to get undressed and drop into bed.

What was going to happen? Would I survive? Did God know what He was doing?

Dad lay still for a few minutes. He felt lost and lonely. He silently prayed. "*I need some reassurance, God.*" He sat up again and picked up his Bible from the bedside table. The pages fell open to the 10th chapter of the Gospel of Mark. The section subtitle caught his eye: "The Little Children and Jesus."

> People were bringing little children to Jesus for him to place his hands on them, but the disciples rebuked them. When Jesus saw this, he was indignant. He said to them, "Let the little children come to me, and do not hinder them, for the kingdom of God belongs to such as these. Truly I tell you, anyone who will not receive the kingdom of God like a little child will never enter it." And he took the children in his arms, placed his hands on them and blessed them. (Mark 10:13 16 NIV).

Dad got tears in his eyes. He knew God was speaking to him. Years later he told me that coming across this passage right then blew him away. He felt comforted. He decided he could trust God when it came to his new son, whether I lived or died. "God loves children," he said. "And no matter what happens, God loves my son."

We would spend more than the next two decades proving that to be true.

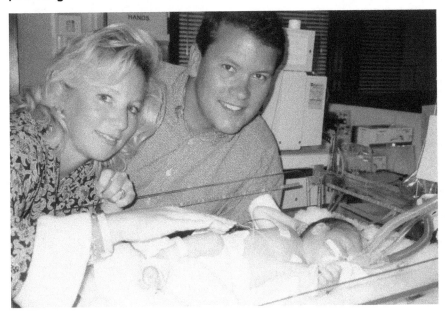

Chapter 2

IT'S ALL RELATIVE

Before I formed thee in the belly I knew thee.

— Jeremiah 1:5 (KJV)

When I graduated from high school, I received a gift that meant a lot to me. In a box was a pair of surgical scissors with blades so tiny they could split a hair. They were high-grade titanium, and on the handle was engraved the name RECTOR.

On September 14, 1995, Dr. Fredrick E. Rector used them to save my life. For the first of many times.

That morning Dr. Rector had talked to my parents in Mom's hospital room and gotten their signatures. After he left, my mother and father just lay there on her bed. They didn't know what to do. So, they called their family.

My father's parents, Ruthie and Bill Mestdagh, and my mother's folks, Marlene and John Boll, all came from all over the city as fast as they could.

"It will be all right," said Grandma Mestdagh, whom I've always called Ma. "You'll see."

"Of course it will," said Nani. That's what I call Grandma Boll. "God's going to bless this little guy."

Everyone was teary-eyed, just the same.

The door opened. In walked Dr. Rector again. The room got silent. Dad stood up.

"He's good to go," said Dr. Rector. "His heart is strong. And his lungs and kidneys are good, too. Surgery is at 5 p.m."

My grandmothers remember to this day what Dr. Rector did next. He pulled them into the hall and looked stern.

"Now ladies. You need to get it together," he said. He wasn't being mean, just blunt. "You have to be strong for your kids."

After other friends and family came and went, Mom and Dad finally had time to themselves. Everyone thought they looked like they were doing okay. But on the inside, they were scared. They held each other for a long time.

● ● ●

My father remembers staring at Dr. Rector's large, big-jointed hands. They looked like they belonged to a farmer, not a surgeon. "How's he ever going to be able to operate on a tiny 5.2-pound newborn?" he wondered. But Dr. Rector had been a pediatric surgeon for more than 20 years, and he was a master at it.

Using the tiny titanium scissors and special 2.5-power magnifying glasses, Dr. Rector struggled for four and a half hours to fix the defects I had been born with. At least the ones they knew about at this point.

First on the list was making it so I could breathe and swallow food.

First, the TEF—when the esophagus and the trachea (the windpipe) are conjoined—had to be corrected. They're designed to be completely separate, and a blocked windpipe would mean I wouldn't be able to get oxygen to my lungs and would suffocate.

Also, my upper esophagus did not connect to the lower esophagus and the stomach. This situation is called esophageal atresia.[1] The esophagus is the tube that carries nutrition from the mouth to the belly, so obviously it had to be able to do its job.

Dr. Rector could not know the extent of these malformations when he made an incision in my tiny torso. Through an opening about the size of a nickel, he delicately explored the anatomy, sorting out just what the problems were. X-rays right after birth in the NICU the night before revealed a lot going on and suggested that the esophagus was sealed off, where it should have been connected to the stomach. The procedures to fix all this were very complex.

While he was at it, Dr. Rector inserted a temporary feeding tube that went through my nose to my stomach. That way I could have nutrition while everything was healing.

Now I would be able to eat and breathe. That was good! But there was that problem at the other end of my body. I had no opening for poop to come out of.

The condition is called anal atresia, or an imperforated anus.[2] It's actually not that rare. One out of every 5,000 infants is born with a misplaced or blocked rectal opening. It may or may not mean that there are other things wrong inside.[3] In my case, we would learn in the next decade or more that I did indeed have a lot more internal problems. A lot! But for now, Dr. Rector made another way for the body waste to come out. He created what's called a colostomy.[4]

This is how Dr. Rector did it. He disconnected my colon from the rectum. Then he rerouted two ends—they're called stomas—to little holes he made in the abdominal wall. That's where the waste would exit my little body, for now.

It was awesome, really. Not the way the ugly red "double-barrel" stomas looked, sticking out of my little abdomen, or how much of a mess the colostomy created (just ask my parents!). But the fact that modern medicine can do what it does and save lives—that's awesome, isn't it?

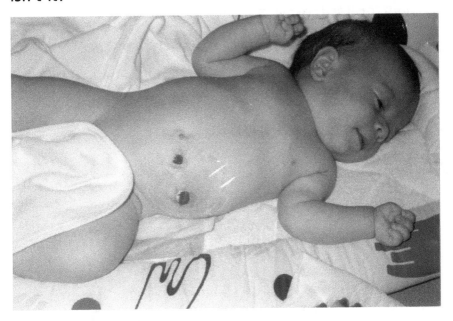

Because if I had been born not too many years earlier, I would have died.

● ● ●

For the third and last time that day, a very tired Dr. Rector walked into my mom's room. Dad and Mom were anxiously awaiting news of the operation.

"How did it go?" my father asked. He was holding Mom's hand.

As you might guess by now, Dr. Rector is kind of matter-of-fact. But, he cares a great deal about his patients. We would grow to love him, and he and his wife, Anne, became life-long friends. But he can be very straightforward. He was that night.

"It was a success, yes. But, he was the toughest kid I've ever operated on! In 20 years!" he said, slumping into a chair. "It was like sewing wet tissue paper together!"

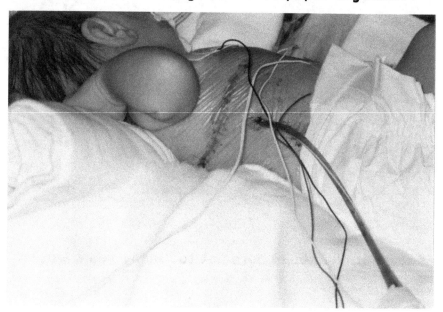

He talked with Mom and Dad for another 20 or so minutes. My folks remember it was the first time anyone mentioned something called VATER syndrome.[5] Then he gave my folks his home phone number and said to call if they had any concerns.

If they had concerns?

Mom's devotional reading that day was called "The Cure for Resentment." She said it couldn't have fit the situation better. She was reminded that it does no good to ask God why. *Why me?* He's God, after all. He knows everything. The past, the present, and the future. And He loves us.

So, she and Dad knew God was going to take care of us. And all of the suffering and pain and limitations and struggles were going to have a purpose.

Still, the unknowns weighed on my parents. They had been dreaming of a baby for a long time. Now there were so many questions. What was this VATER syndrome? Was I ever going to be a normal little boy? Would I have health problems all my life? Were they strong enough to be my parents?

● ● ●

Early the next morning, Dad came back to St. John Hospital. His first stop was at the NICU to check on me. He told me later he was feeling a little sorry for himself. Here he was, a new father, having to adjust to the idea of a sick son. Plus, the NICU was an intimidating place. There were beeping monitors, pumps, and machines everywhere. The light was dim. Visitors had to put on a pale green gown and wash their hands before entering where the sick babies were.

That's what he was doing when he overheard some people talking quietly. He glanced over and saw a young couple and a man he assumed was a physician.

"We can take care of the arrangements for you," the doctor was saying to the man and woman. "Or, if you know of a funeral home you'd like to use, we will work closely with them."

My father froze. He felt a lump rise in his throat and tears filled his eyes. He instantly knew this was a turning point for him. His perspective shifted from self-pity to gratitude.

Those sad parents had just lost a child. No matter what happened, Dad and Mom would be thankful. Because I was alive.

Chapter 3

HEADLAMPS AND LAUNDRY

Do not pray for an easy life; pray for the strength to endure a difficult one.

— Bruce Lee

During the first few days after the surgery Mom would come to visit me in the NICU. Before she could say hello, though, she had to lie down on the tile floor.

When they accidently punctured the membrane around Mom's spinal cord during the epidural, it made her spinal fluid leak out. That caused the pressure in her brain to decrease, leading to a rocking-bad headache.[1] The only way to relieve her horrible pain was to lie completely flat. (If the pain didn't go away in a day or so, medical staff would administer a "blood patch," which is sort of like a plug in the hole. Mom needed a patch twice!)

But, she had to visit her newborn son, of course. So, she would slowly make the trek from her hospital room. By the time she got to the Neonatal Intensive-Care Unit, her head felt like it was going to explode. She had to lie down or she'd scream.

Thanks, Mom, for all the pain you endured for me! You and Dad taught me a lot about pushing through difficulties and focusing on the positive. It's been a good skill to have!

After being on the NICU floor awhile, she would feel strong enough to stand again and come to my incubator. I know she longed to hold me. But, I was hooked to a bunch of tubes and beeping machines that monitored stuff like heart rate, oxygen, respiration, blood pressure, fluid levels, and temperature.

When I was born, my parents hadn't picked a name for me yet. They had thought about naming me after my father, but he didn't want to saddle anyone with being a "junior." The day after I was born, though, they had to come up with a name so that Dr. Rector could operate on me. So, they just went with it. The nurses posted a sign above me that said *James Thomas*. Mom even started calling me Jimmy in her journal.

A few days later, though, my mom's parents were visiting the NICU. My grandfather, Papi, walked in and said, "So, how's little JT doing?"

It stuck. No one has called me anything else since. In fact, later, in school, if a teacher called me James, I didn't even think to answer.

● ● ●

I finally got to go home September 28, 1995, 15 days after I was born. Mom and Dad took a video of the car trip along Lake Shore Drive. I looked pretty indifferent, but Mom and Dad were excited! One thing for certain: No one knew what was coming. What I had gone through in the first two weeks of my life was going to seem like a cake walk.

The adjustment at home was, well, a little rocky. To begin with, there was that double-barrel colostomy to take care of.[2]

Back then, the supplies for someone with a colostomy were pretty generic, as in one-size-fits-all. Which means they did not fit a baby, especially a newborn.

The ostomy[3] pouch was as big as my entire tummy. It had to be folded and tucked to keep it under my clothes. Even though Mom and Dad would wash and dry the area with a hair dryer and put a special powder on the skin, the adhesive that held the bag in place would loosen.

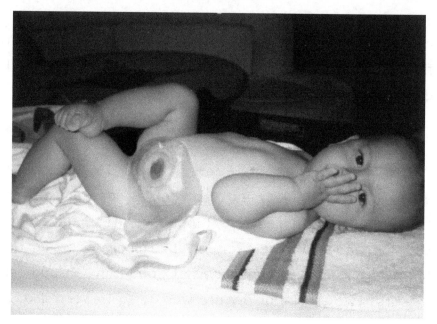

Plus, how do you keep a baby from moving? The whole system would crease and gap, and you-know-what would ooze out.

Not fun! Irritated skin and rashes. Constant laundry. Change after change after change, all through the day and night. And stinky! Sometimes if Dad needed to clean me up in the middle of the night, he would put on his headlamp so I'd stay asleep. As Mom said then, this "became our new normal."

Mom and Dad had been assigned a specially trained nurse at St. John Hospital for support. They called her the Colostomy Queen. She got lots of calls from my folks.

This went on for months. In a diary entry dated November 11, 1995, Mom wrote, "The new bag didn't work well. We went back to the Little Ones [brand]. . . Bad news. This bag even broke. Yikes! We are discouraged."

One time my mom was so frustrated and fed up she called my dad at work, crying. "You've got to come home and take us to the hospital! This is not working!" she said. "We have to talk to the Colostomy Queen—now!"

When Dad came to pick us up, Mom climbed into the back of the car with a big towel around my oozing middle. All she said was, "Just get me there!"

Since they'd only talked to the Colostomy Queen on the phone, they didn't actually know where her office was. The receptionist gave the best directions she could. Down to the basement, turn left, then right . . .

By then I was fussing—okay, screaming—and my parents were upset and anxious and tired. They pushed through a final door they thought was the right one.

No. It wasn't the right one. It was the morgue.

"May we help you?" a confused attendant asked.

Mom burst out crying.

Really?! Dad thought. He put his arm around Mom. *Do we really need this, Lord?*

Then they started to laugh. Definitely a tension breaker! And, a reminder that I was not *in* the morgue, praise the Lord!

They finally found the Colostomy Queen, who was very sympathetic. She suggested a few new techniques that seemed to help. Then my folks got the heck out of there.

● ● ●

God sent an angel to help—in the form of a fearless 15-year-old babysitter who became like a big sister to me.

If you thought it might be tough to find sitters who were willing to deal with leaking colostomies, you'd be right. In fact, my folks had such a hard time that Mom asked the people in her weekly Bible study to pray for one!

Someone there recommended Sarah Kennedy, and she was, as they say, a godsend.

Sarah just seemed to take charge of stressful situations and not get bothered about whatever nasty thing was happening. And there were a lot of them when it came to a wiggly baby boy with a colostomy, daily enemas, constipation, occasional asthma, bronchitis, and a bunch of other stuff. Sometimes Mom and Dad would come home and Sarah would be wearing something from Mom's closet, because her clothes had been, well, messed up. Nothing phased her.

She wrote in a college essay a few years later that "it was heartbreaking to see such a young child go through so much pain."

She also wrote that she learned some important things from taking care of me. "This made me realize that not all children are blessed with perfect health and that not everyone is willing to help them out," she wrote.

She also said "the qualities that I accumulated while caring for JT helped me to gain perseverance in life. I will carry this attitude on throughout my life and it surely will help me through the tough times, just like those of my little friend, JT."

Sarah became part of the family. To this day I call her my sister. I even got to be in her wedding.[4] Thank goodness she wasn't the last of the angels we encountered along the way, but she was a favorite.

Chapter 4

PERFECT A**HOLE

Kid, you'll move mountains!

— Dr. Seuss

Good thing we lived only a few miles from St. John Hospital. I spent a lot of my first year of life there.

In early February 1996, I had to be hospitalized for a bad urinary tract infection. In March Dr. Rector repaired two hernias[1] in the groin area. He also fixed a large fistula between my rectum and the urethra. The urethra is the little tube from the bladder to the outside world.

Mom says my urinary system was like a highway with lots of unwanted exits leading to dead ends. "There were like two dozen fistulas in the urethra canal," she said. "You're supposed to have one route. Instead these detours kept showing up. Dr. Rector had to fix those, too."

No relation to the hernia operation, but afterward, my esophagus sounded more and more like a bark. I developed asthma, and then had to go back into the hospital because of pneumonia.

Mom and Dad were doing the best they could. But things weren't cooperating. My insides were screwed up. They simply were not working as God had intended them to.

● ● ●

One of the reasons my insides were not working was because that's what can happen to people born with VATER.

VATER syndrome, or association, is actually a bunch of birth defects. The name is an acronym. Each letter stands for a category of possible defects. Some are life threatening. Some can make life difficult, all the way into adulthood. Some are more just annoying. None are fun.

V is for vertebral abnormalities, or bad things happening in the spine. A is for anal atresia, a missing or malformed anus. T and E are for when something goes wrong with the trachea and the esophagus. R is for renal (kidney) defects.

In the two decades since one of my pediatricians, Dr. Ewells, came to Mom's hospital room and confirmed with my folks that I had been diagnosed with VATER, researchers have added two other possible defects to the list: cardiac (heart) problems, and limb abnormalities.

Now the condition is most often referred to as VACTERL syndrome, because of an expanded list of conditions.[2]

People get diagnosed with VATER/VACTERL if they have at least three of the birth defects. It would turn out that I had five.

● ● ●

It wasn't all pain and mess and frustration. There was lots family fun and laughter. We spent my first Christmas at my Papi and Nani's home in Colorado. And in February we traveled to Florida to spend time with them on their boat, where I had my first-ever swim in a pool. (That took a bit of figuring out. With my gigantic floppy ostomy bag hanging off my stomach I couldn't wear your typical baby swim trunks!)

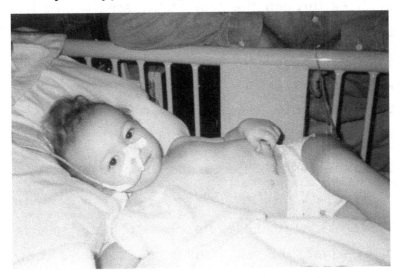

But at the end of summer Dr. Rector decided it was time to try to do what is called the "pull-through" surgery. If it was successful, I wouldn't need a colostomy anymore. In fact, Dr. Rector said I'd be like "all the other kids on the block."

The formal medical name of the operation is *modified posterior sagittal anorectoplasty* (also known by the initials PSARP).[3] It's also called the Peña procedure, after the world-famous surgeon who developed it.[4] My parents didn't know Dr. Albert Peña at the time, but he eventually would be key, not only to my surviving all my congenital challenges, but also to being able to have a decent quality of life. He also became a dear friend of my family. But I'm getting ahead of myself.

Here's what happens during the Peña procedure.[5] The surgeon slices through the skin of the area where the anus is supposed to be, but isn't. Then he has to go hunting for the sphincter muscle—if there is one—that had not connected during development in the womb. After that, the sphincter is pulled down and sewn to the newly created anus.

At a pre-op meeting, Dr. Rector did not give my folks a ton of hope that the surgery would go well.

"I don't even know if he developed a sphincter muscle while in the womb," he said, "and if he did, I don't know if I'll be able to surgically connect it. I'll just have to do my best."

My mom nodded. "There are a lot of people praying for you, Dr. Rector. We will be praying too. God has His hand on you."

● ● ●

On a muggy August 27, 1996, my parents waited for what seemed like half a day in the surgical waiting room at Children's Hospital of Michigan in downtown Detroit. When Dr. Rector finally came to talk to them, he was grinning.

"Today I made a perfect asshole!"

Yes, he really said that.

Dad laughed. I think Mom smiled a little. "Did he have a sphincter?" asked Dad.

Dr. Rector said, "Yes, he does and it's a good one!"

With a sigh, my mom said, "What a miracle and an answer to prayer. . ."

The colostomy had to stay in place until my new "fanny," as my mom called it, healed. Dr. Rector also inserted a thin tube through my abdomen into the bladder to temporarily divert urine. So, for the next month I was crawling, climbing, and starting to walk—all while dragging around an ostomy bag and a suprapubic cystostomy catheter. Picture that.

While I was still at the hospital, our dear family friend, Grace Fenton, came to visit. My Nani and Papi were there too, along with my parents. Mrs. Fenton is a music teacher and she always seemed to show up at my hospital room at the right time, usually bringing cool toys. This time she brought with her this neat thing called a Hoberman sphere. It's a colorful circle of links that expand into a giant interlocking ball.

She remembers noticing a new atmosphere of hope in the room. "Everyone was happy," she said. "There was a sense that things were moving along."

Unfortunately, not everything would be moving along as it was supposed to. But, we'll get to that.

● ● ●

Before Dr. Rector could take away my colostomy, the sphincter muscle had to be ready to take over its pooping responsibilities for an almost-one-year-old. My sphincter muscle had never been used so it is like any muscle, it needs to be stretched slowly, twice a day, every day to allow a passage way for my stool. So, each week the tool (it's called a Hegar Dilator[6]) got one size bigger. We did this for eight weeks. I have to say it was grueling, but it was a must.

For Mom the process was more than grueling, it was torture. The experts say that the baby is supposed to feel only some pressure or a little discomfort. *Not pain.*

But I got to the point where I would start screaming the moment I saw her reach for the dilator. Everyone thought my parents should hire a nurse to help so that I wouldn't associate the pain with my parents. However, Mom and Dad did not want to hand off this sensitive care of their kid to anyone else. They did what they had to, every day.

Once we got past that stage, Dr. Rector was ready to "reverse" the colostomy. On November 7, 1996, he reconnected the two ends of my colon that had been sticking outside my body, preparing my "plumbing" for a return to "normal" operation. At least that's the outcome my parents understood would happen.

While I was still at the hospital, it was Mom's turn to spend the night. November 8, 1996, around 10:30 p.m. Mom said I woke up with my eyes looking bright in an odd way, and restless. The nurse thought it might be a drying effect of the morphine I was on. I kept getting more agitated. A little before midnight another nurse said maybe the pain was getting worse, but they'd have to wait until 12:30 a.m. before administering more morphine.

Then at 12:20 a.m. I started to have a seizure. Mom ran for a nurse, called Dad, and then dialed Dr. Rector. I seized for two minutes, she said, "with blue lips, foam at the mouth, and a stiff body." Dr. Rector came from his home as soon as he could. He moved me to the ICU, ordered blood work, a chest X-ray and called in specialists.

I seized again around 3 a.m., and this one lasted for five minutes. Medication stopped it. They decided one of my lungs had filled up with fluid and then collapsed.

The next day I was stable. After a week of recuperation my bottom and I came home.

When it was time to take out the stitches of the new anus on November 21, Dr. Rector was out of town. His partner, Dr. Paul Stockmann, did it, and told my parents he had "never seen such a good butt."

Then things got really awful.

Chapter 5

THE ROTTEN KID

With God all things are possible.

— Matthew 19:26

At some point during the difficult months of 1997 and 1998, Dr. Rector started calling himself the Rotten Kid Inspector. Guess who was the Rotten Kid?

He was kidding, of course. But my parents weren't the only frustrated ones when it came to my condition. It seems like every time Dr. Rector or his colleagues fixed something in me and thought maybe that was all, they'd discover a new problem.

What was supposed to be simple was complicated. What was supposed to go right, went wrong. My Papi summarized it by saying, "His plumbing just isn't working!"

One explanation might have been that they didn't yet know the extent of my abnormalities. VATER/VACTERL association had only been a recognized diagnosis starting in the mid-1970s. Twenty years later, when I came along, the medical establishment was still just beginning to recognize and understand the rare condition. In fact, Dr. Rector had seen only a few patients at this point.

So, it was daily trial and error. There definitely were trials, and, through no one's fault, there definitely were errors.

● ● ●

"Okay, my sweet JT. You're home now, and you're going to be able to go potty all by yourself. Isn't that wonderful?"

My mother was getting me settled in the nursery. It was a week or so before Thanksgiving 1996, so I was a little more than a year old. I had healed from the Peña procedure and the colostomy reversal. Mom and Dad had brought me home from the hospital, having been told that my plumbing was now going to work "like everyone else's" and we could get on with life as a growing toddler with two loving parents.

Remember what I said about nothing ever going as expected?

Mom still vividly recalls the situation: "After the pull-through surgery when things heal, you wait to see the digestive system start up, literally for the first time. So, you pray for a bowel movement, as strange as that sounds. Well, we did get a bowel movement, and we were all like, 'It worked! Praise God!'" she said.

Now the passage way was open from one end to the other and things could pass through. "Unfortunately, everything was loose and very, very acidic, so JT had what Dr. Rector called a 'fire-engine red' fanny for a very long time," Mom said. "Meaning, his bottom was so raw that it would bleed, and he couldn't sit down. And if he was playing and had a bowel movement, he would stop and just scream."

The runny stuff was followed by extreme constipation. Part of the problem was that I was born without peristaltic muscles[1] to push food along. From esophagus to anus, nothing but gravity pushed food and waste along.

This defect would be a source of much difficulty as I grew up and even into adulthood. I had to learn to take small bites, chew forever, and drink tons of water. Still, food like bread and rice would get caught in my esophagus.

And it's why I had to have regular enemas and then sit on the toilet for an hour at a time. That's a tough thing to ask of a one-year-old boy, but I would play with Legos and Matchbox cars and do art. My parents or Sarah or another babysitter would sit and play, too.

There were no good weeks during 1997 and into 1998. There were good days, but each week presented new, difficult issues.

Months and months piled up with pain and infections and mess and Senokot laxative and enemas and stomach aches and bloating and balloon catheters and baths to soak my bum and trips to the hospital and pleas for other options. My fanny hurt so bad I didn't want to sit. Taking baths was my only relief. Dad would help as often as he could, but Mom was like a prisoner in her own home. She couldn't exactly take me out for a play date or an afternoon in the park, you know?

But, of course, it wasn't just a lifestyle problem. When a body—especially an infant's—doesn't absorb nutrition properly in the small intestines or can't get rid of toxins via the large intestines, there are multiple and far-ranging systemic ramifications. I was jaundiced, lethargic, and not growing.

• • •

With the nonstop diarrhea and testing and infections and constipation, I had by age three spent more than 250 days in the hospital.

The Rotten Kid Inspector kept trying to figure things out. In checking for the cause of the constant constipation, Dr. Rector brought me into the hospital and gave me an enema using something called Gastrografin, an X-ray contrast medium. It's a very irritating solution, even when diluted. He said I did not pass the Gastrografin for more than 24 hours, which stumped him. It made me so sick I had to be admitted to the hospital. They put me on IV fluids and flushed out my colon "almost as a lifesaving maneuver."

Dr. Rector also gave me barium enemas. They outline the rectum. He wanted to see how "decompensated" the colon was. I would throw up the barium. My digestive system and lack of peristaltic muscle were really causing me a tough time.

He also put me under to have a rectal biopsy, because he wanted to make sure I didn't have something called Hirschsprung's disease. That's when parts of the gastrointestinal tract have no ganglion cells and therefore cannot function. Waste collects and the colon swells to become a "megacolon." The good news was that I had ganglion cells. The bad news was the cause of the problems was still unknown.

● ● ●

None of Dr. Rector's testing pointed to what was wrong with me. He thought that was rotten. And he was thinking deeply on how to fix that.

Soon after, Dr. Rector sent a letter to a renowned pediatric surgeon and expert in anorectal malformations and VATER/VACTERL treatment, whose name my parents had come across and asked him about: Dr. Alberto Peña.

"Dear Dr. Peña," he wrote, and began to summarize a long description of my medical situation. "I have not encountered a child with such profound constipation in 25 years of practice. . . If you have any ideas or thoughts that could help this family, they have the resources to come and see you."

Chapter 6

MEGACOLON

Challenges are what make life interesting and overcoming them is what makes life meaningful.
— Joshua J Marine

"Grace?"

Our family friend Grace Fenton heard my mother's voice on the other end of the telephone line. It was late September 1998. Mrs. Fenton knew my parents had taken me to see a new specialist on Long Island for another battery of tests and treatments.

"Kristine? What's wrong?"

Mrs. Fenton will tell you that my mother seldom asks for help. Both Mom and Dad are private people and they don't like to burden anyone, even long-time friends. That's why Mrs. Fenton knew right away that if Mom was calling during a tough time, it wasn't for a girlfriend catch-up.

"JT's not doing well at all, Grace. It's been really hard on him. He's not fighting back," Mom told her. Her voice dropped. "There are no smiles."

Mrs. Fenton knew right then that things must be worse than Mom was letting on. She told Mom that she would pray for me and would ask the church to pray. That wasn't a token gesture. We attended the same church as the Fentons, Knox Presbyterian in Harrison Township, Michigan. My folks believed and had seen that God answers prayers.

But, Mrs. Fenton also knew, as soon as she hung up, that she was going to book a flight to Newark International Airport and get to the Long Island Jewish Medical Center in New Hyde Park, New York, as soon as she could.

She brought along her daughter, Hope, who had babysat me a number of times. It was early Saturday, October 3, when they showed up at Schneider Children's Hospital, the part of the LIJM complex I was in. (Schneider is now the Cohen Children's Medical Center of New York).

No one was in the room with me when they peeked around the curtain. I was pale and sallow. My eyes were half closed. Mrs. Fenton says I looked like I was hanging on to life by a thread.

"Oh, JT, you've gone somewhere," she whispered. "Come back to us."

● ● ●

Dr. Rector heard back from the renowned pediatric surgeon to whom he had written. Dr. Alberto Peña said he would be happy to confer with my parents. Dr. Rector encouraged them to explore the possibility and I'm grateful they did. Dr. Peña would become crucial to my health and quality of life. And like Dr. Rector, he would become a friend.

We would learn later that Dr. Peña tried hard to not say no to requests for consultations, because he knew that if families had discovered him and were willing to travel far to see him, they likely were desperate for help.

We flew in August 1998 to New York. Dr. Peña, at that time, was chief of pediatric surgery at Schneider's and professor of surgery at Albert Einstein College of Medicine, which also was located at Long Island Jewish Medical Center. He had become famous in medical circles for his innovative approaches to colorectal problems— he had treated thousands of children from all over the world with colorectal malformation problems.

The months leading up to my hospitalization on Long Island had been traumatic for everyone. Dr. Rector and his colleagues were trying everything they could think of to help my messed up intestinal tract. My parents made appointments with a chiropractor, a reflexologist, and a massage therapist. They tried herbal therapy.

They even took me to a "motility" center.[1] Nothing made a huge difference. My bowels were stuck.

In fact, the colon was getting stretched out and weakened like an oversized balloon that never went back to flat. It was developing into a "megacolon."[2]

We felt immediately comfortable with Dr. Peña. Maybe that's not surprising. He had been a pediatrician and pediatric surgeon for four decades. He knew kids! Also, he was very empathetic to how families suffered. Part of his motivation to specialize in pediatrics was because as a young father he had lost a toddler son to biliary atresia—a rare condition that today might have been survivable.[3] Plus he was a really, really nice man.

At that first consultation on August 10, 1998, Dr. Peña ordered some tests and then said I needed a sigmoid resection. The megacolon was a threat to my life. But, no one imagined that Dr. Peña would need to remove 18 inches of colon from my little three-year-old body.

The surgery, on the afternoon of September 27, 1998, lasted five hours. The sigmoid area of the colon is the section of the intestines right before they become the rectum. A resection means to cut out an unhealthy section and reconnect the remaining parts.

Dr. Peña made an incision from the top of my chest to my belly button. What he removed was one of the largest megacolon sections he had ever seen.

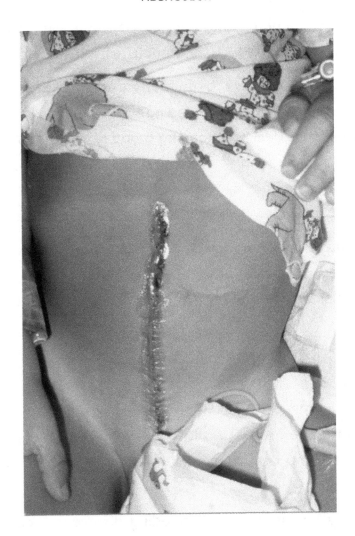

● ● ●

That night Mom and Dad had a *déjà vu* experience. I had a seizure, just like two years before, right after the surgery to reverse my colostomy. This one lasted a minute and a half. They raced to call Dr. Peña and he came right away, ordering a dose of the medicine Ativan and sending me to PICU, the Pediatric Intensive Care Unit.

The cause may have been dehydration and a severe electrolyte imbalance leading to hyponatremia, a condition that occurs when the blood level of sodium, an electrolyte, is abnormally low. Dr. Peña just shook his head, because he had done the same procedure on hundreds of other patients, with no such reaction.

A few days later I moved back to a normal hospital room. I seemed to have a little more energy, but I was emotional and actually told my parents, "I want to go home!"

That wasn't going to happen for a few more weeks, though. We first had to tackle Dr. Peña's "bowel management" program.[4] That basically meant days and days of experimenting with every method possible to figure out the best way to keep the colon moving and cleaned out.

Every patient is different, needing different "cocktails" of laxatives, enemas, and so on. We had so many X-rays to check for results we lost count. (Dad teased that I was glowing.)

It was trial and error—and *frustrating*. My "output" was liquid-y, so Mom and Dad had to change my diapers just about *every hour*—even at night. No one was getting much sleep.

That's when Mrs. Fenton and Hope came to visit. No wonder I looked "gone."

But seeing them—and seeing the cool toys they brought—lifted my little-boy spirit. My face lit up and I smiled from ear to ear.

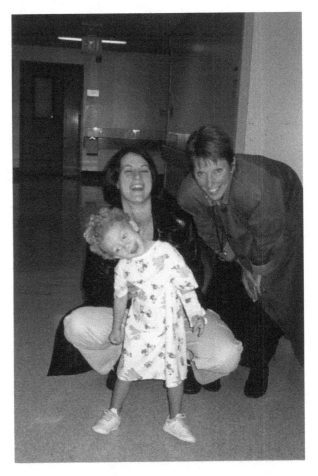

That's when my mom and dad walked back into the room after taking a break. They were surprised and glad to see Mrs. Fenton and Hope. But, they were even more thrilled when they saw me.

"He's back!" Dad said.

That would turn out to be one of those premature statements, but Mom and Dad were grateful it was true at that moment.

Chapter 7

THE JESTER

The most wasted of all days is the one without laughter.

— Poet e.e. cummings

My parents hurried into the Post Operative Care Unit. When they spotted my bed, they were concerned to see not one but three nurses huddled around me.

"What's going on?" my dad asked. "Is something wrong?"

All three nurses turned. They had grins on their faces.

"Your son is so funny!" said one of them. "Most kids wake up after an operation crying. Not JT. He is always giggling and cracking jokes!"

A second nurse nodded and chuckled. "He's such a jester!"

Mom and Dad looked at each other, eyebrows raised, not really knowing what to say.

"Hey, Dad. Knock knock . . ."

My father smiled. "Who's there?"

Soon after, my folks found a book they bought me: *The Jester Has Lost His Jingle*, by David Saltzman.[1] Colorful toy jesters began to appear as gifts in my hospital rooms from this point on. (I still have quite a collection!) My family would name one of their boats *The Jester*. It was a label that stuck.

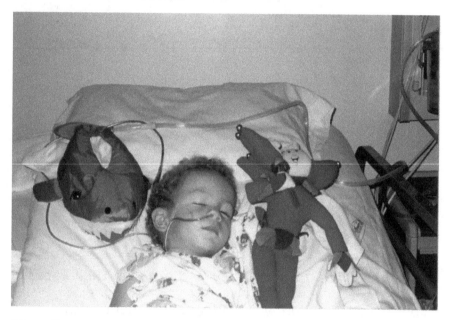

"Boo."

"Boo who?"

"Oh, don't cry, Dad. It's just a knock-knock joke. . ."

• • •

My parents tell me that I wasn't one to feel sorry for myself, even at this young age. I guess I had a natural tendency to be positive and think of other people.

"Dad, is that kid sicker than me?"

We were still at Schneider's on Long Island, recovering from the intestinal resection and bowel-management program. My folks had started taking me out into the hallways and waiting areas in a Radio Flyer red wagon. Pretty soon I could take short walks. It was good to get outside my room and interact with kids.

"Yes, I think so," Dad replied. He and Mom remember that even at age three I would look in on other children and smile at them and try to cheer them up.

We took a few more slow steps, and I peeked into another room. "That kid isn't as sick as me, right?" I said.

I was learning about my world and learning about myself. I eventually came to realize everyone is going through something. Your challenge may be tougher than theirs, but that doesn't matter. For them, their difficulty is real, and deserves your patience and compassion.

The time on Long Island also meant I was surrounded by children who had colorectal problems like me. Kids from all over the world came to see Dr. Peña. That made me realize I wasn't the only one always feeling nasty, doing enemas, taking medicine, sitting on the toilet, and sleeping in hospital beds far from my bunny and my dog.

That made me feel good inside. Inside as in my heart, not inside my belly. <Grin.>

● ● ●

No, not *inside* my belly! At least not yet. Yes, getting rid of that monster megacolon was supposed to help me feel better and get things moving. But, everything—everything—moved slowly.

On Sunday, October 4, 1998, Mrs. Fenton and Hope went back to Michigan. It also was the day Dr. Peña made two announcements.

First, he was ordering the stop of enemas and the start of Senakot. Maybe this new oral laxative would get things going.

The second piece of news made me happy. I was going to be discharged from the hospital! I could stay at the nearby Ronald McDonald House of Long Island with my parents. (They had been staying there all this time.) Meanwhile, Dr. Peña and his staff would continue trying to figure what treatments I needed. We would still have to walk to the hospital every morning to get X-rays, but we could spend time together again.

My grandparents, and my Aunt Lora and her children, Justin, Jaco, and Casey, came a few times to visit. That helped cheer us up. One afternoon Dad, Mom, and I went into Manhattan to visit Central Park and the zoo. (We even went with Mom to Soho to shop!)

Ronald McDonald Houses[2] do their best to create a warm, homelike environment for ailing children and their families. The Long Island setting had a wonderful large indoor play area. There were always children to play with. Sometimes we didn't speak the same language, but that didn't matter. On warm days we'd go out in the back patio area, where there were play structures and toys too.

But, imagine if you (as a child) woke up each morning feeling as if you were going to be sick and throw up— you just didn't know when. You'd have good and bad moments, but all day long you felt nauseated, your stomach ached, and your butt was raw. It would be hard enough if you were in the comfort of your own home. But, you weren't. You were suffering in a strange place.

I was surrounded by kids going through this—and my parents were surrounded by fellow parents and family members of all those kids.

My mom says that one of the few good things about my medical challenges was that they brought her and my father into contact with hundreds of people from countries and cultures they otherwise would not have been exposed to. They got a chance to share the love of God in small ways, even if it was just listening or offering encouragement.

"God knew the Mestdaghs were not the type to go off to some faraway place to be missionaries," Mom said to me. "Instead, He sent us to nearby places!"

"Such a rare birth had us search out doctors from all over the country that could help us. So, we kept finding ourselves in different Ronald McDonald Houses, meeting people from all over the world. We all had the same things in common: sick kids and time! We'd pray together and witness to God's love," she said.

"It has been a beautiful experience to see these families come together at such trying times in their lives."

● ● ●

Unfortunately, the physical part of things didn't seem to progress much. Diaper changes throughout the night; wet stools, gas pains, stomach aches, daily X-rays, and just not feeling good—it all seemed endless.

One morning, Dad woke up upset. Another tough night, another bad start to the day. He had had it. He walked to Schneider and asked to see Kathy, the main nurse in charge of my situation. He told her we just weren't making enough progress. She was sympathetic, but asked Dad to be patient. Progress *would* come, she said.

That just wasn't what he wanted to hear. The ordeal was really starting to wear my folks down.

After all, they had come to New York, thinking it was for a couple of weeks. It turned out to be more like two months. They had hoped there would be an end to what they (and I) had endured for three years. Instead, it was three-steps-forward, two-steps-back waiting and wondering. They never knew what the next day would bring. Or, how many more days there would be.

It started to drive my easy-going dad crazy.

"You run at a fast pace in your regular life, and then you have to switch gears to slow mode, because there's nowhere to go except from the Ronald McDonald House to the hospital and back. Day after day . . ." Dad remembers.

Several weeks into their stay, my parents started to notice funny noises outside the RMH. Human noises, but not normal stuff, you know? "Odd laughter, crying, yelling, mumbling," Dad said.

His curiosity got the best of him. "You couldn't see anything over the fence, because of the trees and shrubs. So, I climbed up on the playground equipment in the Ronald McDonald House yard to see what was going on," said Dad. "Then it became very clear what the source of the sounds was."

We laugh about it now, but back then, the irony was painful.

Who would have expected the Ronald McDonald House to be next door to a psychiatric hospital?

As days became weeks, Dad began to joke that he felt he was ready to check in to the Zucher Hillside Hospital and join the patients there. Luckily, we got some good news before that happened.

I was finally going to be able to go home.

Chapter 8

MEMORY GAME

I am not afraid of storms, for I am learning how to sail my ship.

— Louisa May Alcott

Anne and Fritz Rector's doorbell rang. Anne opened their front door and looked down.

"Can Fritz play?"

I was four now. When my family decided to move, they discovered a Grosse Pointe Shores home for sale next door to the Rectors and bought it. That meant I could come over all by myself to see if Fritz had time for a game. This kind, but very busy pediatric surgeon and his wife, would spend hours with me. We built bird houses, made bullets, and put together model cars, planes, and boats. I loved it. I think they did, too.

Our long driveways were side-by-side. My parents had given me a little motorized toy car (our family loves cars!), and I would drive it around the driveways. Anne said I would take colored sidewalk chalk to mark up the area like a parking lot.

"He would draw a blue handicapped place next to the garage. He was unusually observant for a child that age," she said.

I guess it's understandable I would know you put handicapped parking spots close to a building. I certainly had a lot of experience with them by now.

A favorite game was called Memory. It's like Concentration, where all the cards from a deck are laid face down and you have to remember which cards are where so that you can match more pairs than your opponent.

Fritz and I would sit on the floor around the coffee table, with Fritz folding up his very long legs next to my very short ones. Sometimes Anne would join us. When I think about it now, I realize how patient they were with me.

Anne says playing Memory turned out to be ironic, given what we would soon discover about how my brain is wired. (We'll get to that.)

"Maybe that was the appeal. Here was a memory game that he could be good at. He could remember that much, and he enjoyed remembering," she said. She also said I was "very competitive, and he loved beating Fritz."

I am, and I did. I could beat Fritz at Checkers, too.

● ● ●

During the years I was age three and four, I had battled pretty much the same kind of stuff as I had the previous years. I was reacting badly to the laxative Senekot, so Dr. Peña told us to stop using it, and to resume daily enemas.

That wasn't good news for my folks. "It's tough to get a child to lay on his side, period," recalls my mother, "but then also to insert liquid, have him hold it for a while, and then sit on the potty for an hour. . .? Every single day? That's REALLY tough."

All this was in addition to the typical childhood viruses, infections, and accidents. And one time I was so sick I had to be admitted to St. John Hospital. No tests revealed what was going on.

Then my pediatrician, Dr. Ziegler, was walking the halls and remembered my family recently had been in Colorado. "Has JT been tested for giardiasis?" he demanded.[1]

That was it! For a change there was an outside cause of an illness. Giardiasis is an intestinal infection caused by a microscopic parasite often found in water where wild animals live—and poop.

In the fall of 1999, Dr. Peña performed my 12th operation, a hernia procedure. Apparently, that jester came out in me again, telling jokes in the recovery room, even though I was crying from the pain. I do like to make people smile.

Right around Christmas things got really bad, with diapers needing to be changed every half hour and me so constipated I was vomiting diarrhea (sorry!). Dr. Peña ordered an antibiotic, Flagil, and my tummy bloated. Mom says she and Dad put me in a bathtub and catharized me to reduce the air in my belly. This went on for days. What a way to end 1999.

● ● ●

The years 2000 and 2001 were a little better, but not event-free. Every day I had potty accidents at preschool and then kindergarten. I'd be out of my school uniform (because it got soiled) constantly, and kids would ask why. I remember always saying "I sat in water." I'd confess at home: "Mom, I lied."

I would need to carry kid-diapers in my backpack. Once a little girl saw them and asked, "Do you have a baby at home?" Again, I lied and said, yes.

The accidents were upsetting. I was embarrassed, and I felt different than the other students. They also were creating disruption on the playground. Kids can be cruel. There are always bullies in any school. Even though I was eager to learn and wanted to be among other children, I struggled. Part of it was the bathroom issue, yes. But, there was something else.

● ● ●

My mother still remembers picking me up from preschool one afternoon in the fall of 2000. I had just turned five and was proud to be attending the Grosse Pointe Academy Montessori Early School program. As the longest continuously operating Montessori program in Michigan, it was very highly regarded.

The line of cars in front of the school was moving slowly, so Mom took advantage of the moment to point to some classmates and ask me their names.

I recognized the kids, but I could not recall any of their names.

In fact, I could not tell Mom my teacher's name. I could not recite the lyrics of the simple songs the class would sing. I could not remember, after raising my hand to answer a question the teacher asked, what the question actually had been. I could not remember the beginning C letter of a word like CAT by the time I got to the T.

I could not even say the alphabet.

My dad says that even at age three I could remember everything I saw, and I could recall directions to places where I had been. But, regardless of this, it was beginning to be evident that there was something different about my brain. I could not memorize.

Now my parents and I were faced with two areas of challenges to deal with: the medical and my soon-to-be discovered severe learning disabilities.

When my parents approached my preschool teacher with these observations, she dismissed them as the temporary shortcomings of an active little boy. When things did not improve, they arranged a conference with the Head of School, who merely said that maybe the school was not right for me.

Mom and Dad were stunned at the lack of willingness to explore the possibility of learning differences. So, they agreed, the school was not right for me. They immediately left to apply at another top-rated institution, University Liggett School.

The results at ULS would be mixed and would lead to major upsets and changes in both the school and my life.

But, at this point, all I wanted to do was be like other kids, and learn to read.

Chapter 9

FOREIGN COUNTRY

I think a hero is an ordinary individual who finds strength to persevere in spite of overwhelming obstacles.

— Christopher Reeve

"It's like one day the light switch is on and one day the switch is off."

It was September 2002, the end of the first week of school. My first-grade teacher, Peggy Dettlinger, was on the phone with my mother. She already was seeing alarming signs when it came to my ability to learn.

"He is an absolute delight, Mrs. Mestdagh. He never complains or acts out. He sticks with something and always tries to do his best. But. . ."

My mother was not surprised at what she was hearing. Still, frustration and fear started to grip her heart. "What is causing this, Mrs. Dettlinger? What can we do?"

Mrs. Dettlinger, who now serves as University Liggett School's Assistant Head of School, as well as Head of Lower School, told Mom she didn't have an answer—yet. "Please continue to read to him at home and encourage him to connect words to things in his life. I'm sure we'll figure something out."

But, weeks went by and I made little progress. I could tell you my letters, but I couldn't "blend" them together into words. I couldn't even remember the first letter I had just read before moving on to the second or third. Once-a-week tutoring didn't help.

By the time January 2003 parent-teacher conferences rolled around, Mrs. Dettlinger was stumped. (In fact, she says her experience with me motivated her the following year to take a class on learning disabilities. She eventually got a master's degree in special education.)

"JT was the first child in my 15 years of teaching I didn't know what to do to help," she remembers. "All my methods didn't work. It was heartbreaking."

● ● ●

Other people in my life began to notice things, as well. My grandparents, Papi and Nani, were visiting my parents one day, and Papi made an off-hand comment that struck everyone as true.

"It's like JT is in a different country."

In one way I was a normal little boy who loved his toys and swimming and hot dogs and hugs from his grandparents. In another way, though, I was like someone traveling in a foreign nation—someone who can understand when people speak, but reading the signs and menus and books? Clueless.

Just as they were in the realm of my medical needs, my parents became proactive. They sought help from a variety of professionals for my still undiagnosed learning challenges. They would learn, though, that the experts had no magic solutions. In some cases, they had no practical solutions, either.

That spring, my school referred us to a well-respected educational psychologist. Dr. Marquita Bedway did the battery of tests everyone in the psychological-educational industry uses to try to figure out what is wrong with a kid and what to do to fix him or her.

For example, Dr. Bedway reviewed my records, observed me in my classroom, and interviewed my teacher and my parents. She had me take a whole bunch of tests: the Conners teacher rating scale; the Bender Gestalt Test; the Achenbach Child Behavior Checklist; the Behavior Rating Inventory of Executive Function; the Wechsler Intelligence Scale for Children-III; the Wechsler Individual Achievement Text, 2nd ed.; and the Wide Range Assessment of Memory and Learning (WRAML).

Man, it was tough for a rambunctious eight-year-old who couldn't read and was overwhelmed by tests. My parents tried to make it fun and I tried not to complain.

Dr. Bedway's long report would be a comparison basis for many other evaluations in the years to come. It would launch what seemed like endless examinations, meetings, interventions, and debates that went on for at least a decade. Years of hopes raised and dashed.

She wrote that my "general cognitive ability" was within the "high average range of intellectual functioning." My "nonverbal reasoning abilities" were "superior." But,

> JT's abilities to sustain attention, concentration, and exert mental control are a weakness relative to his verbal reasoning abilities. Mental control is the ability to attend to and hold information in a short-term memory while performing some operation or manipulation with it. A weakness in mental control may make the processing of complex information more time consuming for JT, drain his mental energies more quickly as compared to other children his age... [Also,] his weak performance on the Symbol Search subtest was below that of most children his age.[1]

When it came to reading, spelling, or mathematics, my scores were borderline or low average. Yet my functional IQ was 115.

Here's one statement that stood out to my folks. Dr. Bedway was interpreting the results of the WRAML test: "His pattern of scores suggest that too much of a language (semantics) component compromises his ability to remember."

I simply could not remember words. Numbers were a problem too.

● ● ●

What were her recommendations? What should my family and I do? What should my teachers and the school administrators do?

Here is some of what Dr. Bedway recommended, and the results:

- "JT should be taught decoding skills through a highly structured, multisensory, phonics based approach. . ."

  [She wrote that Orton-Gillingham method is often effective. That would prove to be not true in my case.]

- "Given his strong visual skills . . . JT can develop compensatory strategies to facilitate word recognition."

  [She suggested flash cards, labeling objects, using word recognition computer programs. They only were marginally helpful.]

- "Active working memory weakness is associated with difficulty blending phonemes. He will benefit from an instructional approach that highlights prefixes, suffixes, compound words, and word families. . ."

  [Unfortunately, my school's curriculum did not have the same focus.]

- "Close monitoring of JT's reading progress is recommended. . . A comprehensive reading evaluation should be completed within the year. In addition, a full re-evaluation that addresses attention and memory is recommended by the end of 3rd grade."

[The evaluations occurred; in grades 1-5, unfortunately, there was a gap between recommended accommodations and what actually was put in place.]

Dr. Bedway suggested I should be evaluated by an audiologist and a speech pathologist. She also told my parents to take me to my pediatrician, Dr. Ewles, "to address possible inattention problems." (On top of everything else, was I ADD? It's now known to be part of a condition that has three forms: ADHD Inattentive Type or what was formerly known as ADD; ADHD Hyperactive/Impulsive Type; or ADHD Combined Type. It would not be until college that I was given an actual ADD diagnosis.)[2]

● ● ●

In the United States, if a child in public school needs special education services, he must have an Individualized Education Program (IEP). The federal law, known as the Individuals with Disabilities Education Act (IDEA), says public schools must create an IEP for every child in the district receiving special education services. It's a legally binding document, for non-private schools.[3]

Here are some of the things an IEP must include.

• A statement of the child's "present level of performance."
• The child's annual education goals.
• The supports and services the school will provide to help the child reach the goals.
• Modifications and accommodations the school will provide.

- How and when the school will measure the child's progress.

But here's a crack that a lot of kids fall through: The law doesn't require private schools to provide special education services.

Public school districts are required by IDEA to set aside some funding for special services to students in the private schools within their districts, but it's very limited. And, everything depends upon the cooperation of the private school.

● ● ●

In December of 2003, the Grosse Pointe Public School System agreed to evaluate my need for special services. The evaluation confirmed Dr. Bedway's findings and what my folks and my teachers knew. My educational achievement was very low.

What were the district's recommendations? The IEP document—the first of many—ordered "preferential seating," modified assignments, oral testing, and longer time for tests.

That was all they recommended. But even these accommodations would meet resistance in my private school's administrative offices. My parents' battle had just begun.

Chapter 10

LEARNING TO FALL

If you aren't failing, you aren't trying. If you aren't trying, you aren't succeeding.

—Anonymous

My new ski instructor looked old. You know, old like my parents. He had a funny accent, too. But even at eight years old I loved learning from others, so I was willing to try anything.

My parents had hired a previous instructor, a nice guy in his mid-20s, every time we came to Beaver Creek Resort in Colorado. But this year, when he said he had a scheduling conflict, we suspected he had gotten tired of having to deal with a kid who had bathroom challenges. No one blamed him.

So, the ski school assigned us an instructor who was new to the resort, a man from the Czech Republic. His name was a tongue twister: Ladislav Lettovsky. Luckily, his nickname was easier: Ladi.

It turned out that Ladi was a whole lot more than a certified alpine instructor. Good thing we got along, because—after my father and my grandfathers—Ladi would become one of the most influential men in my life.

● ● ●

I wasn't a never-ever, a first-time skier. As soon as I could walk my dad stood me on his skis in front of his legs and gave me little rides around the bunny slopes. I had my first lesson at age two. Can you tell my parents love to ski? But they didn't force me to learn. I loved it, too!

My grandparents, Papi and Nani, had built a ski-in/ski-out home in Beaver Creek Resort when the community was just starting. We spent Christmases and other holidays and school breaks there, sometimes with family and friends, sometimes by ourselves.

My first visit was Christmas 1995, when I was three months old. Mom and Dad asked my babysitter, Sarah, if she would come with us for a week. At first, her mother hesitated. After all, Sarah was only 15, and they had lost Sarah's father when she was four. Mrs. Kennedy didn't want to lose anyone else. But Sarah begged, and she gave in.

So, Sarah came to Beaver Creek with us—and she kept coming every Christmas for the next eight years! What great memories of skiing together, of ice skating, roasting marshmallows, playing games. No wonder I consider Sarah my big sister. And, like me, she thinks of Colorado as her second home. We love Michigan, but, well, Colorado is Colorado.

Sarah remembers pulling me around the resort in a sled, bundled up in a blue snowsuit. Or, we'd get in the snowcat, a cabbed vehicle on tracked wheels that reminded me of a tank. We'd ride it up the mountain for lunch at Beano's Cabin with my folks, who would be skiing all morning. Then Mom would bring me home for my treatment, and Sarah could take a few runs with my dad before the slopes closed at 3:30 p.m.

By the time I met Ladi, my skills were pretty basic, but I was easily cruising down the blue trails. Being out there in nature—where no one asked me to take medicine or get tethered to IVs or try to read or recall someone's name—made me feel like a normal kid.

I had begun to realize I was different. On every trip to the bathroom I was reminded my body did not work right. Every day at school I felt frustrated at not being able to read, embarrassed at failing spelling quizzes, and anxious at being called on and not having an answer.

But being in nature untethered me! It lifted my spirits and gave me confidence. And the best thing? Being outdoors made me feel closer to God.

There was one skill I had to get good at first, though. How to fall.

● ● ●

"Watch me, JT."

Ladi had taken me high up the mountain on Drink of Water lift. (It's been replaced by the Red Buffalo Express.) It was fun to follow his blue jacket to the front of the lift line—instructors get to take cuts—and have the *liftie* wave us through to the chairs.

On the way up Ladi had told me what we were going to do. I looked at him. Was he serious? *Practice falling down?*

He looked very serious.

It didn't sound like it was going to be fun.

Now we were standing in the bright sun in an area of soft snow near a small berm, or snowbank. All of a sudden, Ladi did a forward roll. He landed on his back, his poles like twigs in the snow, and his skis formed a giant X.

"See, JT, it doesn't hurt."

Ladi brushed back his blond hair and clicked his boots together like a soldier. That aligned his skis. Then he grabbed his poles, let his legs fall away from the berm, and bam! He was up. With a big grin on his face.

"Your turn!"

It may be easier for an eight-year-old boy than a grown man to do a forward roll with skis on, holding poles. But it still felt awkward. Once I landed on my back, Ladi pulled my skis together, which snapped my boots together. Then he pushed my legs over, rolling me on my side. That got my skis under me and I could push myself up.

"See, you did it!"

We repeated the maneuver a couple of times, getting very damp, and then moved to a steeper hill, where the snow was thinner and the ground harder. You aren't always going to land in powder, right?

By now we were laughing. It had become a game. We changed it up a bit. Fall and stand. Fall on the other side and jump up. Fall twice in a roll and then get up.

Before you knew it, we were rolling down the hill on skis and people were looking at us like we were crazy.

Did I say this wasn't going to be fun?

"So, JT, falling is nothing to worry about. Whether when skiing or anything else," Ladi said, sitting in the snow after the last roll. "It's like being willing to fail at something new. That's the best way to learn."

Ladi then said something about "muscle memory," which I eventually would come to understand. "Over time, falling becomes second nature. Your body takes over. It still can be scary. If you aren't a little scared, you aren't trying hard enough. It's just that you understand what's happening. See?"

● ● ●

From that point on Ladi and I were pals. I could tell he liked me. He treated me like a son. Never like a patient. And he made everything he taught—even the most challenging and rigorous activities—enjoyable.

Ladi is a very, very smart man. He analyzes everything and thinks outside the box. He has learned English as an adult; embraced a new way of life in America; earned an MBA and a PhD; raised three children with his wife, Martina; done business all over the world; and has taken calculated risks as an outdoorsman. Yet one of his dominant philosophies is that life must be fun.

If you have fun while you're learning something, Ladi says, you'll gain the skill or retain the information more quickly and thoroughly.

No wonder I was drawn to him.

It's been that way now for 15 years. We have skied and gone skinning throughout the backcountry, ice-climbed at night, hiked to high-elevation huts, scaled summits, trained in avalanche preparedness, bobsledded, kayaked, and mountain-biked. And we've put our sights on new heights overseas (see the Epilogue).

All these adventures have, yes, been fun. But, looking back, I now realize that in every moment of every outing Ladi was looking for ways to grow, and to help me grow.

Now when I'm faced with an obstacle that I think might trip me up, I picture what Ladi would do. When I feel anxious about a new medical procedure or new challenge in life, I remember what Ladi taught me.

Whatever you fear, break it into pieces, or steps. Then build a skill for each stage, and practice, practice, practice. That will give you confidence for the next challenge.

I was going to put this into practice a lot in the next few years.

Chapter 11

JT'S STAR

The time is now, the reason is you.

—Dr. Nido R. Qubein

"It's a terrible idea."

Dad was sitting with Mom at the kitchen table. It was the fall of 2004. I was nine, and still struggling in school. They were discussing whether to let me be in a Christmas play at church. Dad was leaning against it. Leaning hard.

"JT would have to do a lot of reading and memory work. Why would you ask a little boy with terrible short-term memory, who can't read, to do that? And then put him on a stage?" He frowned. "That is a set up for failure!"

Mom had a different perspective. "Yes, I know, but remember. We said we weren't going to protect him. If JT wants to do it, I say we let him."

She smiled. "And after all, it's Knox. Everyone there knows and loves JT."

Every Christmas, our home church, Knox Presbyterian, offered the community an original holiday production about the coming to earth of our Lord and Savior Jesus Christ. This year's script needed a child to play the part of a sick kid named Sam. That sounded like me.

One problem: What Dad said was true. I still couldn't read. I could hardly recall my friends' names. How in the world would I be able to memorize dialogue and then recall it on stage? Not only that: I also would need to sing a solo.

Maybe we should do what Dad suggested: Have him hold the script and a little mic while in the audience, and be ready to whisper into an ear piece in my ear if I forgot my lines!

● ● ●

When my parents asked if I wanted to try out for the role, I immediately said yes.

That was like me. My third-grade teacher, Mrs. Brown, said I was always volunteering for things. Even if I couldn't remember the question I had raised my hand to answer. In regard to the play, too, I really didn't know what I was getting into. But, I loved to do things that might help people. And a play about Jesus might help someone, right?

I also liked to imagine I was a police officer or a firefighter. What child doesn't? Grace Fenton—like my nurses when I was little—said I was always mimicking people and making jokes, which was unexpected from a very sick boy. The jester. That was me.

Friends such as Thomas and Andrew and I would create worlds in a little storage closet next to the stairs leading to the third floor. We called it Fort Five. My parents let us paint it in camouflage. We loved being soldiers and police and spies.

But that sort of make-believe didn't require you to memorize words that someone else had thought up. The Christmas play was co-written and co-directed by Mrs. Fenton, who was Knox's director of music, and by Dennis E. North, who was going to play the father of the kid in the play. It was called "Becker's Star."

At the "Becker's Star" table-reading—the first time all the cast got together to read their parts in one sitting— my mom sat with me and read my lines to me so that I could say them at the right time. There weren't many. But still, this wasn't school or my hideout, and I was surrounded by adults.

Sam, the boy character, was in the hospital on Christmas Eve. Another patient was Mr. Becker, a lonely, unbelieving man. My "pretend dad" would visit me, and Mr. Becker would overhear us talking, reading the Bible together, and praying. Eventually, Mr. Becker would be moved to accept the true meaning of Christmas.

But first, I had to learn my lines. And I had to memorize and sing a song by myself. Would my father's fears come true?

● ● ●

I am surrounded by darkness. I'm alone on the stage. I'm feeling a little anxious. I'm in brand-new red pajamas and slippers, clutching a little blanket. There are hundreds of people looking at me. My family. Both sets of grandparents. My grandparents' friends. My friends and their families. Schoolmates. My school teachers, my golf instructor. Fritz and Anne Rector. But the audience is completely dark, so I can't see any of them.

I know, though, that my parents are out there, praying for me. At home they had read the script to me over and over. They had played the music and taught me the lyrics of my solo. Then they had attended every rehearsal. They would attend every performance.

Up to this point in the first show, I had done just fine and hadn't been too nervous. I had remembered my lines! In fact, I knew everyone's lines. And when I wasn't speaking, all I had to do was pretend to be asleep. I could do that!

I look up. One of the spot lights is shining down. It looks like a star. It reminds me of the Star of Bethlehem.
It's time for me to sing "Happy Birthday, Jesus."[1]

"Happy birthday, Jesus.
I'm so glad it's Christmas
All the tinsel and lights
And the presents are nice
But the real gift is You . . . "

The previous year at *SpringHill Camp I had given my*
heart to Jesus. I feel as I sing that I am telling the truth.
Singing the truth.
Still, I'm glad when the song's done!

● ● ●

My resource teacher, Mrs. Ginger, later sent me a note.
She wrote, "You sang like an angel, but better than that,

you sang the words right from your heart! Everyone could tell that you really love Jesus!"

I hope that is true. That is how I felt. And it wouldn't have happened if my parents hadn't been willing to take a risk, trust God, and spend hours and hours with me practicing!

That's what my stage dad, Dennis, acknowledged in a note to my parents:

> He really made the show work and that wouldn't have happened without your courage and hard work—helping with lines, getting him there on time—just loving him through the whole thing.

At the end, my dad called it a "character- and confidence-building experience."

Maybe for us all.

"It's clear that God did this," my mom said. "There is no other explanation."

Chapter 12

ILLITERATE FOR LIFE

Don't give up just because of what someone said. Use that as motivation to push harder.

— Zig Ziglar

Mom and Dad stared down at the gray IEP documents on the table in front of them. Gray like the small school district meeting room. Gray like the fall day outside.

This wasn't the first time my parents had been faced with an Individual Education Program (IEP) report full of jargon and checklists, but it hadn't gotten easier. There, in black and white, was the bland, heartless evaluation by educational experts of their son's unexplainably disappointing performance. My unexplainably disappointing performance.

The meeting that year, in 2005, had begun in a positive atmosphere. Everyone greeted one another as friends. After all, they had interacted together for years. Some were neighbors.

On one side of the table sat my parents. Hopeful. Apprehensive.

On the opposite side of the table sat the head of the University Liggett Lower School and its special education teacher, plus my third- and fourth-grade classroom teachers. Next to them sat the Grosse Pointe Public School District learning specialist, speech pathologist, district representative, and school psychologist.

But now, they had all become expressionless. No smiles.

Mom remembers that the dull brown table had no decoration on it. Just a box of tissues in the center.

The public-school psychologist opened the meeting and invited Mom and Dad to follow along as she reviewed the existing "accommodations" spelled out in my previous IEP. Something in her demeanor made my mother's heart start to beat faster.

● ● ●

My parents had poured themselves into finding the right combination of tutoring, practice, motivation, and prayer that would break the code and help me read. They tried every program recommended to us: Orton-Gillingham, Lindamood-Bell, Hooked on Phonics, Discovery Read, and many others. They even hired Mrs. Brown to coach me during the summer.

I tried. I did. But I wasn't making much progress. Everyone was getting frustrated. Including me.

I watched students around me blossom into readers. They could read entire chapter books, while I still struggled with words as simple as "the."

In class, I was always nervous that I'd be called on. When the teacher would give an assignment and then walk around the room to check on how each student was doing, she always came to me last. Every time. Everybody knew that's what would happen, and why. I sat there waiting, dreading, a pit in my stomach, because I couldn't do the work.

And spelling tests? Don't even bring them up. I would spend a ton of time trying to practice for them, and still have the worst score in the class. It was so disappointing.

I didn't do playdates or sleep-overs at friends' houses. Part of the reason was never knowing whether there would be an embarrassing bathroom problem. But everyone wanted to play video games and I couldn't read the instructions. Not even START or PAUSE. In fact, I was nervous going to any new place. I didn't like going to a restaurant, because I couldn't read the menu. I'd just order a cheeseburger. And which restroom was for MEN, which was for WOMEN?

Even though I tried to be upbeat, I felt anxious all the time.

How was I ever going to succeed in life?

● ● ●

The GPPSD school psychologist summarized the results of my psychological testing, and then began to describe what she had seen when she visited my classroom to observe me. My mother's stomach started to clinch. Dad got stone-faced; inside he was fuming.

Then, abruptly, she stopped. What she said next was forever burned on my folks' memories.

"Mr. and Mrs. Mestdagh, it's my conclusion that JT is illiterate and always will be. He will never learn to read. You as a family need to accept that, and to learn how to cope going forward."

Mom's lungs felt like all the air in them had been sucked out. She stared at the psychologist, speechless. Tears welled up. Under the table she grabbed Dad's hand. He sat stunned.

The Liggett principal and teachers had tears in their eyes, too.

The psychologist hurriedly added some comments about there being some good "special schools" for children like me that they should think about.

Dad interrupted.

"JT *will* learn to read," he blurted out, his voice scratchy with emotion, but firm. "We will find a way to help him learn to read!"

The women on the other side of the table looked down, or glanced at each other. No one said anything.

"Well, then," said the psychologist, "I think this meeting is over."

● ● ●

My parents had always been frank with me, letting me know what was going on, medically and school-wise. This was one meeting they didn't tell me about. Not until I was way older.

What good would it do, they reasoned. I still had to go to school. Why face the administrators and teachers knowing they believed *I would never learn to read?*

Mom and Dad refused to accept the public-school psychologist's conclusion. That IEP meeting was a life-changer for them. When all the experts say one thing, and you're a parent and your gut says the opposite, you go with your gut. I'm so grateful Mom and Dad did not give up on me.

They did, though, pretty much give up on the famous reading programs that had failed to help. They kept me doing the tutoring while they hunted for options.

Outside of educational stuff, we did family things, and kept dealing with my medical challenges. I had my dog, Duke, and my family. And I had some friends to hang out with. Thank You, God, for Thomas, Andrew, and others who understood my situation and treated me no different than anyone else.

And I had sports.

It was my first season playing with the Grosse Pointe Red Barons, a community-based youth football program. I was small for 10 years old, but I was tough. At least that's what my dad said.

When Coach Cimm—a nice man named Tony Cimmarrusti—put me at center, Dad wondered if that was a good idea. He said to Coach, "You know he's dyslexic, right? He might not remember what the count is."

We stuck with it, though, and I never missed a call. During practice and at games, I could forget how school made me feel tethered to a big rock that was dragging me down. My parents attended every game and cheered. My grandparents, especially my grandfathers, watched when they could. Even Fritz Rector came to my games, and took photographs. You know how that can be. A little embarrassing.

I loved football, even though I was often uncomfortable physically. But my pigskin career was about to get sacked.

We were about to learn that I was in danger of becoming paralyzed.

Chapter 13

TETHERED

Even though I walk through the darkest valley,
I will fear no evil, for you are with me.

— Psalm 23:4

"Jim, look at JT. Is he limping?"

It was a beautiful fall Saturday toward the end of the Red Barons' season. Mom and Dad were up in the stands, watching as I hobbled off the football field.

For weeks now, my back and legs had been sore—more than usual—and my neck had been twitching, as if I had Tourette's syndrome. I hadn't said anything to anyone. I was afraid the doctors or my folks would pull me off my team. But today the pain was so bad I couldn't hide it.

I slumped on the team bench and shifted my shoulder pads under my red uniform. I saw my folks hurrying down the metal bleachers to the sidelines. I smiled up at them.

"Hey, J," Dad said, crouching so his eyes were level with mine. He often called me "J" or "J man." Mom stood next to him with a worried look on her face. "Did you get hurt in the game?"

"No. I've been hurting for a while, Dad. On and off."

Dad glanced up at Mom.

"Remember, he has a high pain tolerance," she said. Then she looked at me as she finished her thought: "And he doesn't always tell us when he's in pain."

When we got home Mom called Dr. Ziegler. I sighed. I knew an appointment with my pediatrician meant I'd be in for tests, and who knows what else.

● ● ●

"JT, why don't you walk up to the nurses' desk and back."

I headed up the hallway, trying not to limp. Dr. Ziegler had already whacked my knees with a little hammer to check my reflexes and examined my legs and arms for strength. I was tingling and my neck was stiff. I could hardly bend and touch my toes. When I turned around, I saw Dr. Ziegler glance at my father, who had been the one who brought me in.

"Okay, JT, that's good," he called to me. He turned back to Dad. "Jim, I think we have a serious situation here. I think we need to get an MRI done quickly."

In the 10 years I'd been alive, I'd had plenty of MRIs. The magnetic resonance imaging procedure uses a magnetic field, radio waves, and a computer to produce a picture of a part of the body. I wondered what part Dr. Ziegler was worried about this time.

"I don't think we need to bring JT into the hospital today," said Dr. Ziegler, "but I'm pretty sure he has a tethered spinal cord."[1]

I didn't know it then, but that declaration terrified my parents. You wouldn't have known it by looking at them, though. They always appeared calm, something Dr. Ziegler noticed.

Here's why the news was frightening. The spinal cord is like a tube of nerves running from your brain to your lower back, a power cord to your whole nervous system. Tethered cord syndrome (TCS) occurs when the fibers of the cord get attached to tissue around the spine. It can attach in different places for different reasons, but if it's tethered, the cord gets stretched out—and damaged—as the spine grows.

Think of a tight rubber band. It leads to difficulty in bending, all-over tightness, and constant pain. Worse, a damaged spinal cord means nerve damage in multiple places throughout the body. And if it's untreated, it leads to irreversible paralysis.

Yes, the diagnosis meant I was forbidden from playing football and other contact sports like my favorite, lacrosse. A big disappointment for a sports-crazy 10-year-old. But, as throughout all my life, you have to roll with it and learn to stay positive. In the next spring I became lacrosse team manager and enjoyed the game from a different perspective.

For unknown reasons, there's a high incidence of TCS in people with VACTERL association if they've had an imperforated anus. Unfortunately, I was in that category. The only treatment for a tethered cord is surgery. Serious, invasive, and risky surgery.

We got through Thanksgiving and Christmas well, and then my parents met with Dr. Ziegler again. It was January 27, 2006, the week before Super Bowl XL.

That's where my mind was. Not on weird things going on with my spine. My parents didn't have that luxury, though.

Dr. Ziegler sat my parents down for the news. My mother says that when he verified that I had tethered cord, they were stunned. I'd had had *several* MRIs as an infant or child looking for a tethered cord, because of my many headaches through the years. Also, it was extremely "ouchy" for me to stand up straight as I was growing. But tethered cord never showed on an MRI.

The doctor told Mom and Dad that as soon as possible they needed to find a pediatric neurosurgeon, a specialist who treats conditions in children affecting the nervous system—the brain and the spine and spinal cord. They knew they would have to hunt for a specialist they could trust their son's future with.

I didn't know all this, of course, when Mom and Dad came home that day. They picked me up and off we went with our friends, the Stefanis, to the Boll Family YMCA in downtown Detroit. In a week the Pittsburgh Steelers were facing off with the Seattle Seahawks, in Detroit! Tonight, we were going to have a blast at the NFL extravaganza event!

At that moment the only thing I was willing to admit I was suffering from was Super Bowl fever.

• • •

A few weeks later we had plans to meet Papi and Nani for a long weekend at Ocean Reef, a community in Key Largo, Florida. Pa and Ma were driving down from their winter home in Vero Beach to join us. We "boys" were going fishing for sailfish. I couldn't wait!

By then, Mom and Dad had had a consultation with Dr. Steve Hamm, a neurosurgeon at Children's Hospital downtown. Dr. Hamm had walked them through how he would recommend doing the tethered cord surgery, which involved cutting and removing portions of the vertebrae.

Dr. Hamm also ordered two *more* MRIs. He felt he needed to know what was going on at the top of the spine, not just the bottom. He was checking for chiari malformation.

Chiari is a condition in which there's something wrong at the base of the skull, and a portion of the brain extends into the top of the spinal canal. Sounds awful, doesn't it? Chiari can cause a lot of the symptoms I had been having. Luckily the results were negative.

But my symptoms weren't getting any better. My left foot and leg were turning inward, among other things. I tried to just ignore it all.

Mom and Dad decided they needed a second opinion. Our wonderful Dr. Peña had moved from New York to Ohio, to work at Cincinnati Children's Hospital (CCH). Mom emailed him, requesting his advice and a referral.

Dr. Peña suggested a pediatric neurosurgeon named Dr. Kerry Crone. My folks forwarded to Dr. Crone my medical records. Now they were waiting to hear back.

In the meantime, Mom and Dad decided a short fun trip would be good for us all. It wasn't going to turn out as they hoped.

Chapter 14

FISH ON

Casting all your care upon Him for He careth for you.

— 1 Peter 5:7 (KJV)

Nothing was going to stop me from getting on that fishing boat. Not even worse symptoms.

We had flown to Ocean Reef on Friday, February 17, 2006. I was very uncomfortable during the two-and-a-half-hour flight, with pain shooting down my lower back and leg.

The next morning, I woke up and discovered that in the night I had lost control of my bladder. At 10, that sort of thing hadn't happened in a very long time, and it upset me. Mom and Dad didn't tell me what they knew—that that kind of accident is likely to be a sign that a tethered cord condition is turning very serious.[1]

Nevertheless, Dad, Papi, Pa, our mate Shawn Albury, and I pushed off from the dock in the 27-foot Jupiter center-console boat at 7 a.m. I was so excited. No school work, no doctors, no worries—just adventure!

Meanwhile, "the girls"—Mom, Ma, Nani, and some friends of Nani's—planned to relax. The average temperature for that time of year is in the mid-70s, perfect for *poolside* adventures.

First, though, my mother had a call she wanted to make. As soon as she thought someone might answer, she dialed Dr. Crone's office at Cincinnati Children's Hospital. A nurse took down Mom's description of all my new and worsening symptoms and said she would relay them to Dr. Crone as soon as possible. "Someone will get back to you," she assured Mom.

So, the girls went on a golf cart ride around Ocean Reef, laughing and enjoying the sights and one another. Then Mom's cell phone rang.

● ● ●

Shawn was yelling. "Fish on! Fish on!"

We were in two- to three-foot seas about six miles from shore. A beautiful Atlantic sailfish launched out of the sparkling water, dancing on the sea. The tall dorsal fin along its back glistened and waved, yes, like a sail.

Then boom, boom, boom! In a matter of seconds three sailfish were hooked and bending our rods.

Sailfish usually travel together. We were attracting them by trolling with live ballyhoo attached to the lines that run through the two outriggers on the boat. Outriggers look like giant fishing rods sticking up off the sides of the boat. Lines of four rods, two on each side, run through the outriggers. The angler holds the rod and mans the reel.

When the fish, which can weigh 60 to 80 pounds, first bites, it's very strong and powerful. The first task is to pull up the line and "set" the hook in the fish's mouth. Then it starts to "run." It will run the line out for hundreds of feet. The sound is fun to hear. Whizzz!

The aim is to slowly wear the sailfish down. The reels allow drag, or tension, so you don't break the lines. The fish can run out 100 to 200 feet of line. Typically, the captain takes the boat out of gear and figures out which way the fish is running. Then the fight is on, and you back down hard on the fish to get to the leader as quickly as possible. (The leader is the last 15 feet of the line. It's clear and attached to the hook.) It can take 10 minutes or it can take half an hour, depending on the fish's strength.

Dad was at the helm. I was in the bow. Pa and Papi were aft, fighting their fish.

That's when Dad's cell phone rang.

• • •

Dr. Crone had called Mom back himself. After a few brisk questions he was to the point.

"What you are describing to me is nerve damage. JT's tethered cord is causing him a possibly irreversible situation. He needs surgery ASAP. Where are you?" he asked. Mom told him.

"Mrs. Mestdagh," Dr. Crone said, "you need to do whatever you can to get to Cincinnati as soon as possible. It's absolutely essential."

After hanging up Mom sat there for a minute. The implications, the logistics, the danger sent her reeling. She couldn't help but start to cry.

My parents had always tried to keep the grandparents informed, but not with a lot of detail so as to protect them from worrying. This time there was no hiding anything.

Nani and Ma were strong for Mom and encouraged her to call Dad immediately and bring us "boys" back to shore. We were probably an hour out.

Mom remembers, "I took a few breaths. I didn't want to scare JT, so I got myself together to call Jim. He answered immediately and I could tell things were going well on the boat and everyone was having fun, just by his tone," she says.

"Then I said, 'Jim, JT has to get to CCH *now*. His tethered cord has become very bad!'"

Dad, in his *happy voice*, so as to not alarm me or anyone else, had to yell over the engine noise. "We have a triple-on right now and it is extremely chaotic at the moment. I'll call you back!'"

Because there were fish off both the bow and the stern of the boat, going opposite directions, Shawn decided I should clip a buoy on my rod and reel and throw it overboard. That would mark where the rod was, and I could get back to it as soon as Pa and Papi landed their catches. Then Dad backed down on the two aft fish, which helped speed up the reeling-in of the fish.

It took 10 or 15 minutes, and then we returned to my rod. The sailfish was still connected. I landed him. And then we, as my grandfathers did, took a photograph grinning ear to ear and released the fish back into the ocean. They were free again to roam the wild.

Dad called Mom back in half an hour. Unbeknownst to me, we were heading in, but not for more fun.

Chapter 15

LIKE A RUBBER BAND

Tough times never last, but tough people do.

— Dr. Robert Schuller

You have a "sacred" bone at the bottom of your spine. Did you know that?

It's called the sacrum. It's a big triangular bone in the middle of the pelvis. Ancient people believed the soul lived there. (Sacrum comes from the Latin for sacred.)

Of course, I don't think the sacrum houses my soul, but it is a pretty important part of the body. Some people have described the bone like a ball wrapped in nerves. It acts like a circuit board for the nerves that travel down the spinal cord from the brain to their connections: the bladder, lower colon, rectum, reproductive organs, hips, thighs, calves, and feet. Awesome.

Anything going on around the sacrum—not to mention surgery on the spinal cord itself—can affect major areas of the entire body! That's why on February 21, 2006, a lot of people (including me) were praying hard.

By 10 years old, I had had a dozen surgeries that required hospitalization. So being under the knife wasn't the scary part. What was scary was that none of my previous operations were as risky as the tethered cord surgery I was facing now.

• • •

My parents and I had scrambled on to a flight from Key Largo to Detroit early Sunday morning, February 19, after a fun Saturday night dinner with my two sets of grandparents. At least I thought it was fun, because we grilled the fresh snapper and grouper we had caught while out fishing for sailfish. Yum!

Mom and Dad, though, kept watching my every move. Then after dinner they told me we had to get to Cincinnati as soon as possible. That meant flying back to Detroit for one day to pack for cold Ohio and a long hospital stay.

I wasn't exactly happy about it, but they said it would help with my terrible stiffness and pain. That would be a very good thing.

On Monday evening, February 20, we checked into our hotel in Cincinnati. The Ronald McDonald house was full, so my folks had made reservations at Vernon Manor, a once-beautiful old hotel where many famous people had been guests. Presidents like John F. Kennedy, actors like Tom Cruise and Dustin Hoffman, as well as musicians like the Beatles and Bob Dylan.

When we were there, the Vernon made me think of a once-elegant old lady dressed in worn-out clothing. It closed its doors three years later and eventually became offices for nearby Cincinnati Children's Hospital Medical Center.

I didn't give it any thought, though. I wasn't going to be in the hotel much the coming week.

● ● ●

We weren't the only Michiganders at the Vernon. I didn't know it, but the next morning, down at breakfast, Dad had run into family friend Grace Fenton! Without telling us, she also had flown to Cincinnati the day before, to show us support. Mom and Dad kept it a secret.

Around noon we took a taxi to CCH. The surgical waiting room was colorful and full of toys and play equipment. But I didn't feel much like playing.

Then Mrs. Fenton walked in! I was happy to see her, because she always made me laugh. She pulled out funny glasses and we started being silly.

Then it was time to meet with Dr. Crone, my pediatric neurosurgeon, and get ready for the operation. My stomach didn't feel very good. Mrs. Fenton stayed in the waiting room, and my folks and I went through the gray double doors. The nurses weighed me, and read my pulse, blood pressure, and temperature. Then I had to change into a hospital gown, my favorite uniform (not!), and get an MRI.

While we were waiting for the MRI to be read, Dad's cellphone rang. He looked at the screen and handed the phone to me.

I heard Pa's voice. My Mestdagh grandparents had returned from Key Largo to their home in Vero Beach. "Hi JT. We're praying for you!"

I grinned. "Don't worry, Pa. Jesus will take care of me." Although I felt anxious, I honestly believed it.

Later I found out that the priest at Ma and Pa's Florida parish, Holy Cross Catholic Church, met them as they were leaving the sanctuary after praying and lighting a candle for me. Monsignor Richard Murphy promised to pray for me too. He kept my name on the prayer list in the church bulletin for a month, and has continued to pray for me since!

"It is time to go to the operating room," Dr. Crone said, standing in the doorway.

Mom asked for a few extra minutes, and ran to get Mrs. Fenton. "It's time. Come see him."

Mrs. Fenton prayed with me and gave me a hug. Mom and Dad did too, and I took deep breaths so I wouldn't cry.

I didn't know what the outcome of this surgery would be. But I knew I could wake up paralyzed.

I wanted to walk into the operating room. I smiled to cover up my nerves. The nurses helped me up on the operating table. Around me were Dr. Crone, his surgical resident, the nurse anesthetist, and anesthesiologist— all with masks on. Then they put on my "SCUBA mask." That's what I called the anesthesia mask that would put me to sleep.

My favorite flavor of "sleepy-time gas" was watermelon.

"Night night!" I whispered, and started to count. I didn't get far.

● ● ●

Mom and Dad had another surprise visitor during my operation: Anne Rector, my first surgeon Fritz's wonderful wife. She was on her way from Detroit to South Carolina, and made a detour to stop and encourage my folks. She stayed for a few hours and then had to hit the road again.

Dr. Crone made an incision in my lower back. He removed tiny portions of the "wings" of my L4 and L5 vertebra in the lumbar region,[1] right above the sacrum. Then he squeezed in to open the *dura mater* covering the spinal cord, and went hunting for where it was tethered.

When I woke up in post-op, I saw my mother's and father's smiling faces. I was groggy and in a lot of pain, but I immediately smiled too. Then I wiggled my toes! I could feel everything! Not only that, I could feel a sense of release in my spine. That felt so good! Thank you, Jesus!

While I was being transferred into a recovery room, Mom went looking for Mrs. Fenton, who had gone off by herself with her knitting to write in her journal and pray during the three-hour operation.

"Grace, he's out!" Mom said when she found her. "The doctor said the surgery was successful! JT's responsive and has feeling everywhere."

Mrs. Fenton jumped up and hugged Mom. "And listen to this," Mom added. "Dr. Crone said that when he released the cord, it literally shot up, like a rubber band!"

We all were praising God for a successful surgery. Now would come a tough recovery.

Chapter 16

YOU'RE NEVER ALONE IN A HOSPITAL

Never will I leave you; never will I forsake you.

— God (Hebrews 13:5 NIV)

Buried in a pile of school stuff is a little booklet from fourth grade that I dictated and put together for an assignment. It's illustrated with photographs my parents took the week I had my tethered cord surgery (TCS) at Cincinnati Children's Hospital.

Good thing I have it, because I don't remember much about the whole ordeal.

There's a photo of me in my hospital bed, connected to IVs. The date is Wednesday, February 22, 2006, the day after I was operated on. The time-stamp is 2:47 p.m. My eyes are closed. The caption says:

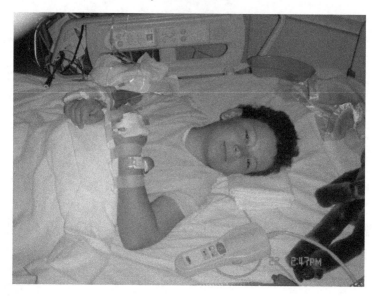

"At this time I am just out of surgery and I had a lot of pain! I did tons of sleeping!"

A second photo catches me staring blankly at the camera. I think I was kind of zoned by the pain and the morphine. I wrote:

> For my pain I had a morphine pump. Morphine is a pain medicine and in the picture you can see the pump. I circled it in red. My left hand has an IV that puts the morphine in my body. In my right hand is an IV, just in case I need a blood transfusion.

You might think that it would be impossible to expect a 10-year-old TCS patient to lie flat for days (to prevent spinal fluid from leaking). Nope. Because my body hurt so much, even with serious pain killers I couldn't bear to move!

Remember, my back muscles had been cut, the vertebrae had been split, and the spinal cord severed. The lights in my room had to be really dim, and people had to talk in whispers. I couldn't stand anyone even touching my bed!

But when people walked in I did try to be cheerful. My parents of course were there. Mrs. Fenton came to say goodbye before returning to work in Detroit. Nurses constantly hurried in to monitor blood pressure, temperature, and medication levels. Respiratory therapists checked my breathing. Nursing assistants cleaned me up and regularly turned my body a little so I wouldn't develop bedsores. You're never alone in a hospital.

● ● ●

That first day went from bad to worse. Another photo in my little book was time-stamped the same day at 7:57 p.m. I have a wet washcloth on my forehead. It looks as if I'm trying to smile a little. But no one was smiling at what turned out to be a high fever.

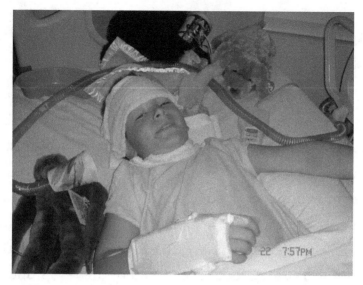

Remember, fever is a response against infection, so the doctors were concerned. They checked my urine for bacteria and ordered a chest X-ray. The pee was fine, but the X-ray showed a thickening of the lungs. Something bad was going on.

Here's the caption I wrote in the booklet for this photo:

> This was a tough day! I had a fever of 103 1/2°. It was caused, because my lungs were collapsing, because I had to lay flat on my back for so long. I had to do a breathing treatment two times per hour and it really hurt.

The fever continued through night. My heart rate kept dropping, maybe because of the morphine. Dad slept in my hospital room with me.

Thankfully, Thursday was a little better. Everything was still painful, but my fever had decreased.

We had a wonderful surprise: My grandmother Nani showed up from Florida for a short visit!

I started to feel more like me. I still needed dim lighting, but Mom says I started joking around with people. (That sounds like me.) She says Dr. Crone was encouraged by my attitude.

I was not in a joking mood when the physical therapist came, though! Having to move was agony! But it ended with a massage. Yay!

The next day, Friday, the PT made me get out of bed completely. It took me 40 minutes. Yes, 40 minutes! Making my body move a fraction of an inch at a time, all the while wanting to scream! Sometimes it hurt so much I couldn't help but yell "My back! My back!"

But I got up.

My reward? Chicken noodle soup for lunch. Ah, a gourmet meal!

● ● ●

After an uneventful Saturday with lots of rest and some walking, we heard some good news on Sunday.

Dr. Crone came in. He was tall and older, like Fritz, and kind and quiet like him, too. Dad and Mom were sitting in chairs around my bed. I had already gotten up and walked three times, once with the PT, once with nurses, and then again with the PT. It wore me out, but it felt good being able to move.

"My patients usually are here at least 10 days, JT," Dr. Crone said. He stood at my bed, and his hand was on my shoulder. "But you are doing wonderfully."

I looked at Dad and Mom. They had hopeful expressions on their faces.

"I am not sure why I am doing this, but I'd like to send you home early, because you are doing so well," he said. He reached down and gently patted my curly hair.

I couldn't help but grin. Home! Boy, did that sound great!

"I know how this happened, Dr. Crone," I said. The surgeon cocked his head. "I have so many people all over the world praying for me— and God was with me and answered their prayers!"

Maybe that surprised Dr. Crone, I don't know. He glanced at Mom and Dad, smiled and sort of nodded, and walked out of the room.

Tomorrow, I would walk out of this hospital!

Chapter 17

MELTDOWN

The only limit is the one you set yourself.

— Felix Baumgartner

Thump!

I heaved my library book up onto the kitchen island, all 478 pages of it.

My fifth-grade class had visited the school library today. We went once a week, and I usually wandered around not knowing what to choose, since I still couldn't read. Today I noticed my classmate Nicholas lugging a big book, and I grabbed the same title.

Even if I couldn't make sense of it, at least I would look like I could, right?

Mom was making me an after-school snack. Her head popped up when I dumped my burden on the counter.

"Wow, JT," she said. She looked at the book and then at me. "That's a big book."

I nodded and looked down. I pictured my classmates bringing books home they actually *could* read and my stomach started to get tight. After all I'd been through— the illnesses, the surgeries, the anxiety at school, the isolation—I was tired of it.

I just wanted to be like everyone else.

"So, JT . . . do you . . . want *me* to read this to you?" Both Mom and Dad weren't big readers, but they didn't let that stop them from helping me.

Mom started to flip through the book. It had no illustrations or photos in it. Just words I couldn't decipher.

She looked a little confused. "Or . . . do you . . .?"

All of a sudden, tears welled up and frustration and fury and pain grabbed me like a giant claw so hard I felt like I was going to pop. I slid to the floor.

"Mom! I don't care anymore if I ever pee or poop like everyone else! I just want to read!"

● ● ●

After my tethered cord surgery in February, Mom and I had spent the spring at my grandparents' place in Key Largo, Florida, to help me recover. My dog Duke came too, and he and I swam together every day. I couldn't run or even walk fast yet, but I was getting stronger. Dad flew down almost every weekend.

My parents had hired a nice teacher named Michelle Beach (isn't that a great name for someone who lives in Florida?) to come twice a week and homeschool me. Mom taught me on the other days. We followed my University Liggett School curriculum. When we went home in May, I finished fourth grade with my class.

The summer had gone by fast, with another great week at SpringHill Camp (I attended every year) and lots of family boating. Then fall. Fifth grade. How I dreaded it.

At the same time, I was facing more medical problems. Turns out I didn't get through the tethered cord situation without permanent damage.

In addition to the daily enemas and constipation, I was diagnosed with something called a neurogenic bladder. The most common symptom is enuresis, and no 11-year-old boy likes a situation in which he is unable to control when he pees.

My wonderful urologist at Cincinnati Children's Hospital, Dr. Pramod Reddy, explained that the bladder is like a balloon. If it gets stretched out, it doesn't go back to its natural size. Mine was permanently damaged by the tethered cord situation.

Now I no longer had the sensation of needing to go to the bathroom. The normal bladder holds around 445 ml of liquid. Mine held more than twice that. My dad said I "peed like a racehorse"—like, literally for a minute.

Throughout the day I had to remember to use the toilet. At night, half an hour before bedtime, I had to make myself urinate. Then I had to do the same thing again 10 minutes before going to bed. The "double voiding" was crucial because if my bladder held any urine during the night, I'd wet the bed. On top of that, Mom would set an alarm for 3 a.m. to take me to the bathroom. A similar "double voiding" occurred in the morning. Otherwise, I'd have problems at school. Embarrassing.

There was talk of another big surgery, a procedure called the Mitrofanoff.[1] But Mom and Dad decided to hold off on it.

For a long time, my chronic medical issues had been uppermost in my parents' minds. It seemed like this VATER/VACTERL situation kept surprising us with a new health crisis. That's why when I had the melt-down in the kitchen, it broke Mom's heart. Not just because it was suddenly obvious how traumatized I was by not being able to read. But, also because she felt terrible that she and Dad—and all the learning experts they had turned to—had not found a solution before it came to this.

● ● ●

Mom dropped to the floor and held me. "We'll figure something out, JT. We will," she whispered.

As soon as I caught my breath and got quiet again, I took my snack and went up to my room and she called Dad.

They now knew they had to put the reading crisis on the front burner.

But how? They already had tried all the best known, most respected reading programs in the nation. They had spent large sums on tutors, and had sacrificed hours and hours of their own time coaching me.

Then Mom remembered Kathy Genthe.

Mrs. Genthe was a friend in Ann Arbor, Michigan. She and her husband, Richard, had dealt with severe dyslexia in their youngest of six children. In fact, all of their children had experienced learning differences. Like my folks, the Genthes also had been frustrated with slow-moving education institutions and ineffective for-profit reading programs.

Then they had stumbled upon a little-known learning innovator based in Denver, Colorado, named Stephan D. Tattum. Steve's reading system had transformed their kids' lives, and is now actually helping their grandchildren.

Despite feeling unhopeful and wary of setting me up for yet another failure, Mom refused to give up. She called Mrs. Genthe.

● ● ●

Mom and Dad learned from the Genthes that Mr. Tattum just happened to be in Detroit right then. He was spending a week training teachers in his system, which at that time was called the F.A.S.T. Reading Program.[2]

Like being assigned to Fritz for surgery the day I was born, and discovering world-renowned VATER/VACTERL expert Dr. Peña, and randomly meeting Ladi, my outdoorsman mentor—the "coincidence" of Steve being in town was clearly God moving in my life.

After dinner Dad drove us 20 miles to Bloomsfield Hills to Mr. Tattum's hotel, what's now the DoubleTree, but then was called the Kingsley Inn. None of us said anything during the half-hour ride on that dark and chilly September night. I tried to ignore the pit in my stomach. This was going to be another disappointment. I would sit down, answer some questions, and let the man assess me. Then he would make worthless recommendations. I had gone through it so many times. I'd leave feeling like a failure once again.

My parents, Mom especially, would later admit to dreading the meeting too. But they also did not believe in coincidences. What were the odds that Mr. Tattum was in not just Michigan, but Detroit, at the same time he had been recommended to us? They had to give him a try.

The dim hotel lobby was empty except for a man sitting in a chair. He had shaggy gray-blond hair and a mustache. Mom would later describe him as looking like a rumpled professor.

The man stood. "Mr. and Mrs. Mestdagh? I'm Steve Tattum." They shook hands. Then he turned to me, got on one knee, and went eyeball-to eyeball.

"And you must be JT. Let's get started, okay?"

As I followed Mr. Tattum down a hall to the room he was using as an office, I glanced back. Mom gave me a little wave and Dad was trying to smile.

An hour later I was the one smiling. In fact, I was grinning ear to ear. After my folks and Mr. Tattum talked a bit and arranged an appointment early the next morning, I practically skipped out of the hotel, jumping with my arms in the air and shouting these words for the first time in my life.

"I can read! I can read! I can read!"

Chapter 18

I CAN READ! I CAN READ!

If you are not willing to learn, no one can help you. If you are determined to learn, no one can stop you.

— Zig Ziglar

From that moment on, my universe changed forever.

The moment I got in the car after that first meeting with Mr. Tattum—from that point we called him Steve—I started phonetically sounding out words. My face was glued to the side window, watching billboards and street signs flash by. I still couldn't *really* read, but for the first time, I tried to.

Wood-ward Av-e-nue, De-troit Zoo, Mound, Hoo-ver, Mor-oss . . .

Steve had kickstarted something in my brain. [1] More than that, my confidence had been switched on!

Later my parents would share with me how they kept glancing at one another in the front seat the whole trip home. Mom said it was like there was a brand-new kid in the car. "Unbelievable," she whispered to Dad.

● ● ●

I, too, was very aware something had changed. It was all the more stunning, because in the first few minutes of the meeting with Steve, my stomach had sunk. It looked as if the meeting was going to be the same old same old.

On the table between us, Steve had placed a flipbook, just like all the flipbooks I'd seen in every other unsuccessful reading program I'd tried. Made of card stock with a spiral binding, the flipbook sat up like a rectangular pyramid, with tabs of letters in bright colors that could be flipped over one at a time to create words. B-a-t. C-a-t. D-e-n. P-e-n.

Great. My anxiety level shot up.

Next he "cleaned up" the way I pronounced consonants and vowels, and pointed to some one-syllable words for me to sound out. I struggled. We worked for about 10 minutes.

Then he picked up the flipbook and tossed it aside. "You'll never see that again."

What? I was surprised (and glad) and remember feeling an immediate sense of trust. This guy was different! Maybe things *could* change.

Then Steve pulled out a rectangular white board about the size of a laptop computer. It had little magnetic tiles of letters scattered all over it. Together we went over what he called the vowel galaxy, sounding out nonsense words. Then he turned over the board.

This side was covered with tiles made up of two to four letters like *un, ex, rupt, mit, ble,* and *tion*—organized in colors. Steve taught me a few of these. This was where I started getting excited.

Later I'd learn that those combinations of letters were called prefixes, roots, and suffixes. Steve moved a few around and pointed to the result.

"Okay, JT. Read that one."

"Un . . . *rupt* . . . *tion*?" I looked up. "What's that?"

"It's a nonsense word. But did you see what you just did? You just read a three-syllable word."

We then read several words like this: un-mit-tion, ex-mit-tion, ex-mit-ble, and so on. Ironically, these were easier to sound out than one-syllable words like tent or camp.

Then he put a book in front of me. I remember the title: *Ocean Fun*. It was one of more than a 100 that Steve had written for his program.

F.A.S.T. emphasizes getting students to read books right away.

He had me try to read a sentence that most first-graders could read: "It's fun in the sun." I made two errors and then he took over for two sentences. We went on like this for a page and a half. *Amazing!*

"JT was reading sentences by himself at the end of the session. That was huge," Steve remembers. "The combination of reading and doing three-syllable words broke the concept for JT that he wasn't a reader. From that moment, JT felt he was a reader, and he was."

He's right! And that magnetic white board would become my magic carpet—to grade-level reading, to a high school diploma, to four wonderful years of college and a bachelor's degree, and to all that has come after that. What a ride!

● ● ●

Steve would later tell us that I had one of the most severe cases of dyslexia he had ever seen in the 30 years he had been working in the field of reading and learning differences. My very poor short-term memory and processing disorder made it all the worse.

But he noticed I didn't wear what he calls a "mask"—a defense system some kids with learning problems (or other challenges) use to cover up what is really going on. Masks can be anger or an "I don't give a damn" attitude, or always acting like a comedian. Or they might just withdraw and become invisible in the classroom.[2]

"When we met, JT was just a kid eager to learn. I thought, 'Boy. You're the kid I wrote the program for.'"

Steve also says he spotted something else.

"JT stood out for his reading issue, but he stood out more because of his emotional intelligence—which is superior to mine, and to most adults I know," Steve would tell my parents. He told himself, "I'm going to help this kid learn to read, come hell or high water."

I had no idea what he meant at the time. I just wanted to read!

● ● ●

Steve tutored me for a week. We discovered I learned better in the afternoon than the morning, when I had low energy and my brain didn't process well.

On that Friday, my fifth-grade teacher called my mother on a lunch break.

"What are you doing with JT?" she said.

"What do you mean?" Mom asked.

"I can't believe it. I gave out the normal classroom assignment. You know, read a paragraph and answer questions," said my teacher. "When I got around to JT, I expected to have to explain everything and walk him through the work."

She paused. "Kris, he had already filled out the worksheet! I asked him how, and he said, 'I read it'! I said, 'what'? And he said it again, 'I read it'! Kris, what's going on?"

That's how motivating Steve's program was. Before, I would have looked at all the letters on that worksheet and not even tried to figure them out. I would have just waited for my teacher. But because of Steve, my attitude had done a complete 180. I wanted at least to try.

When Steve returned to Colorado, my parents arranged to hire a F.A.S.T. tutor. All fall we pushed to learn. When I got out of school at 3 p.m., Mom would drive me 45 minutes to Farmington Hills to work with Miss Susie Jacobs. Then back home for my hour-long medical treatment for my daily bowel management program, then homework, dinner, and off to bed.

The schedule was exhausting, plus I wanted to continue with sports. Then, on a call with my parents, Steve reminded them of Denver Academy.

Attending there seemed too big of a change to my folks. That is, until something big changed.

● ● ●

I was walking down the hall at the end of the school day. Brown and orange paper leaves and turkeys covered the bulletin boards, but I don't remember if I noticed them or what my mind was on or if any of my friends were around. My memory is frozen on just one person.

I heard a man's voice say, "JT! Got a minute?"

My stomach did a flip. No fifth-grade boy wants to be summoned by the headmaster. It didn't even help that the headmaster's golden retriever, which came to school with him every day, stood at his feet, wagging his tail.

"Yes, sir."

University Liggett is Michigan's oldest independent, coeducational school. The Head of School was the top administrator of the Lower School (elementary grades), Middle School (grades six through eight), and Upper School (high school).

He ran the show, and the lives of all the staff and students.

He motioned me over to a corner near a drinking fountain. I remember looking down at the cheerful dog, thinking of my own yellow lab, Duke, and trying not to be nervous.

I don't recall every word the headmaster said, but this is what stuck with me.

"JT, I need to let you know that you're not reading or writing well enough for you to stay at Liggett for Middle School. You can't come here next year."

I felt my face get hot. It felt like this powerful man had ambushed me with that news, just out of the blue. I know that if he had talked to my parents first, they would have warned me.

"Yes, sir."

I turned and walked toward the school's back door, then bolted across the wide field that separated the campus from my back yard. (Our home and the school shared a property line.) All I could think was *I am stupid! I really am stupid!*

By the time I jerked open the little black gate in the fence and ran to the side door of the house I was crying.

"JT! What happened? What's wrong?" My mom grabbed me and peered into my face and looked me all over to see if I was hurt or what. I couldn't answer, I was crying so hard. "JT! What is it?"

Finally, I calmed down enough to tell her. She immediately burst into tears herself and resisted the urge to march over to Liggett right then. Instead, she called Dad and they set up an appointment the next day for a meeting with the headmaster.

The man did not appear. Instead, he sent the lower school headmaster. The decision was already made. There was no discussion.

● ● ●

A door had been slammed in my face. I was devastated, and I know my parents were really upset too. But if we hadn't been forced to leave Liggett then, we never would have experienced a miracle. I know now that that's the way things work out sometimes, if you have faith.

By Christmas break, my parents and I had visited the Denver Academy and applied to enroll me for the spring semester. I was excited to learn I was accepted. In January 2008 my mother and I would be moving to Colorado.

Chapter 19

THE CASTLE DOOR

It's not the mountain we conquer, but ourselves.

— Sir Edmund Hillary

Early one morning Mom and I pulled onto the Denver Academy campus. It was March 2007. Our yellow lab Duke (a girl!), was in the backseat, sniffing the cool air. As I gathered up my backpack Mom surprised me with a question.

"JT, is it OK to be here?"

I didn't know it, but it had been very hard for Mom to agree to move to Denver. Dad had been convinced attending DA was what I needed to do, but Mom had "dug her heels in," she told me later.

The thought of being separated for months from Dad except for weekend visits, of leaving friends and church and both sets of my grandparents, of disrupting everyone's lives—it all seemed too much to her. But Dad said, "We are doing it."

"I had to get my act together," she would later tell me, smiling.

Me? The minute I saw Denver Academy, I knew I wanted to come! The three of us visited during the Christmas 2006 break and everyone we met made me feel like I belonged there. The campus on East Iliff Avenue in central Denver was cool, too. It was a former hospital[1] built in 1898, with beautiful old brick buildings, surrounded by tree-lined quads and courtyards.

So, Mom and Dad had raced to find an apartment in the Cherry Creek neighborhood. They rented furniture, we packed up the car, and Mom and I (plus Duke, but not Dad!) moved in January 2007.

I loved the apartment, because it was in a high-rise building, just like my favorite television series at the time, "The Suite Life of Zack & Cody." Another upside was being close to Vail, where I joined the Vail Ski and Snowboard School and competed every weekend. We also saw Ladi and his family more.

I was sad not seeing Dad every day, but he flew to Denver most weekends and we had a few fun family trips, like visiting the Grand Canyon.

But, on this clear, crisp March morning I looked out on the snow-dusted campus and, unlike all the years prior, I felt eager to start the school day.

"Mom," I replied, "every day here is like going to a castle and I just open a new door."

● ● ●

If you walked through the door of my fifth-grade classroom, you would immediately know that it was anything, but typical.

A different way of teaching, for kids with different ways of learning.

Soft music was playing. Small table lamps and a candle cast gentle light around the room. Framed art decorated the walls. Little water fountains and pots of plants were scattered around the shelves. We had typical school desks, but we often sat on bean bags or exercise balls or cushions. Next to the teacher's desk was a six-foot cardboard tree with a mess of pillows piled beneath.

Mrs. Emily Friend[2] and Mrs. Lisa Petrella were my teacher and assistant teacher. They were wonderful and knew all about kids with learning differences. They also were trained in F.A.S.T.

The day started quietly. All the kids knew the routine: walk in without talking, turn in homework folders, and go to our desks to work on a short project as everyone got settled.

"My assistant and I kept our voices low, but greeted them with smiles and enthusiasm," remembers Mrs. Friend. "I aimed for my classroom to be a gentle beginning to the school day that students could rely on, hoping they felt like they could let their guard down and relax there."

Once the dozen students had arrived, we had Morning Meeting. We'd gather around Mrs. Friend and Mrs. Petrella for character values lessons. Mrs. Friend said that seeing each other eye to eye in a circle was better for what she called social skills practice.

At the end of Morning Meeting each student would pick a kid and said something positive to him or her. That built "a feeling of acceptance and unity, thereby increasing peer-to-peer cooperation and lessening bully behavior," said Mrs. Friend.

After Morning Meeting, she would turn off the overhead lights and light a candle. We could lie down anywhere in the classroom or lay our heads on our desks. Then the teachers would lead us in breathing exercises. We would visualize our worries and fears away (for the moment, anyway!), and "set our intentions" for the day. Then we'd begin lessons!

Mrs. Friend said the aim of these routines was to lower anxiety and stress and make learning easier and more fun. I loved it. I loved learning. My grades showed it. But more than that, I loved to learn how to learn, right alongside kids who also had challenges.

I realized I wasn't alone. We all had something to deal with, but it didn't stop us. The message from everyone, from administrators to custodians, was "You can achieve!"

After just a few weeks, I said to my mom, "I don't feel different here, Mom. Everyone is like me."

At Denver Academy I finally felt like I fit in.

● ● ●

One time the whole school was putting on a Culture Fair. Our classroom was assigned to do a report on Australia. With all the kids working on one project there were a lot of opinions about how we should do it. That meant compromise and being a team player. Not the easiest thing for fifth graders!

As we were getting ready on the big day, a couple of boys and I were trying to set up a life-size cardboard cut-out of Steve Irwin, the late Australian television personality and animal expert known as the Crocodile Hunter. Next to him was a big sign with a digital recording of an Aussie greeting for visitors to the classroom. We were supposed to have our hands free to pass out information. But, Steve Irwin and the sign kept falling over! We were getting frustrated.

I've been told many times that I have strong visual spatial abilities. I guess it's true. At least it's true in this situation, I could see a solution.

I grabbed some objects laying around and engineered a surface with supports in place for all the materials we needed for our display. My teammates gave me high-fives. *Good onya, mate!*

● ● ●

At night in our Cherry Creek apartment Mom and I would call Dad and tell him about the day. At first Mom would go over my F.A.S.T. materials with me as I did my medical treatments. After a while she'd help only if I asked.

One night she overheard me say something to Dad, and she jotted it down on a sheet of stationery. I don't remember saying it, but this is what she recorded:

> "Today was amazing, Dad! I sat down on the computer tonight and I didn't have to have Mom read everything to me. I did it by myself. It is the first time I ever felt like this!"

Chapter 20

THE F.A.S.T. HOUSE

Rise above the noise and keep your poise.

— Papi Boll

You know that idea I mentioned about being in a castle where every day I could open a new door? Well, every weekday morning I opened a door in a small white cottage and had an adventure before my regular fifth-grade class.

The little building was where the old hospital's caretaker once lived. Now it was known as "the F.A.S.T. House"— where Steve Tattum had his office and where kids came for assessment and tutoring in a fun, healing setting.

For the five months that I attended Denver Academy, I would climb the steps at 8 a.m. to the F.A.S.T. House. I'd hang my jacket in a closet in the little foyer. Then I'd sit down in one of the overstuffed sofas or in the rocking chair by the brick fireplace in the main room. The walls were covered with colorful artwork. Light streamed in from the old windows, which looked west and south out on the campus. I loved watching the trees through the little panes of glass.

Next to the front room was the dining room. I remember the old wood floors creaked as you walked. Here flowery wallpaper decorated the room. One wall was painted red. Sometimes the table was used for tutoring, sometimes for office work. My mom and I often would volunteer to help assemble information packets for the F.A.S.T. program. Through the dining room you could get to the kitchen and another room often used for office space or meetings.

If you turned the other way, you'd see French doors. They led into Steve's office. It, too, was anything, but traditional.

For starters, a five-foot high Tyrannosaurus rex greeted you when you came in! It guarded the tabletop jukebox-style radio and CD player, and usually was decorated according to the season. Today it was wearing green for St. Patrick's Day.

There were always other funny things around the office, like a ceramic old lady or a wacky animal. In fact, the whole house was what "Mrs. O" called whimsical, because of Steve's vision to make it fun to learn to read.

Mrs. O was Rosemarie Offenhauer, Steve's assistant and a trained F.A.S.T. tutor. Mom called her "a gift from above." She became a good friend. We had fun together.

Outside the back door was a basketball hoop. Mrs. O would shoot hoops with me as a "reward" or a break between tutoring sessions. She was pretty good!

From the little court you could see a green lawn and then the elementary school quad. The building included a kitchen, which teachers used for celebrations and experiential teaching. Mrs. O remembers baking chocolate chip cookies and oatmeal cookies there with me and some other boys one day after school. Yum.

One day Steve videotaped an interview with me, my mother, and my father in the F.A.S.T. house. He wanted to document how we all felt about my progress and the program.

When he asked me how it was going with my reading and my time at the Denver Academy, I remember what I said.

"It is going great. I can read, I can write, and I feel good about myself."

● ● ●

Now, I heard Mrs. O approaching.

"Hi, JT. How are you today?"

She sat down in the facing sofa and smiled. "I wanted to share with you some good news from Steve. He's sorry he's traveling and couldn't tell you himself. Remember when you came to Denver Academy in January you were reading around the level of a kindergartener?" she asked. I nodded.

"Well, according to the latest tests, you've not only moved up past the first-grade level, the second-grade level, and the third-grade level. You're reading close to what a typical fifth grader would read. Not only that. You're writing four or five sentences all by yourself every night," she said. I could feel myself grin from ear to ear.

"All your hard work is paying off. Isn't that marvelous?"

● ● ●

My mother flew back to Detroit in early April. She and my father had an appointment with the headmaster and teachers at University Liggett to talk again about me and Middle School.

They were so excited to share the progress I had made at Denver Academy. They expected their old acquaintances, the educators to whom they had entrusted their son and who they knew had tried their best to teach me, would be excited too.

The headmaster again did not appear. Instead, the assistant head of Middle School came. Three teachers sat with her as my folks got ready to share my Denver Academy grades and test results that proved my progress.

Mom and Dad reminded them of the F.A.S.T. program. They shared how I could now read at the fifth-grade level—up from well below first grade. Then just moments into the meeting Mom and Dad looked at everyone's faces.

They were like statues. Every single one.

"We aren't here for you to hear about JT's success, are we?" Mom said.

No one said anything.

"Then why are we here?"

Mom says she can't recall the exact words, because they had upset her so much. But she remembers something like this coming out of the assistant head's mouth:

"Due to JT's severe disabilities, he does not fit in with the culture of University Liggett and cannot return here for Middle School."

● ● ●

In a letter to one of my former Liggett teachers, Mrs. Dettlinger, my mother described how one day I asked her if Steve was an answer to prayer. You see, every birthday I would blow my candles out after making one wish: that I could learn to read. Every night I would say my prayers and ask God to help me learn to read.

So, yes, Steve—and his reading system—was an answer to those prayers.

In a few weeks—despite Liggett's decision—Steve and I were going to share that answer back in Detroit in front of a gymnasium full of people who ranged from curious to skeptical.

Chapter 21

FOR THE KIDS BACK HOME

Setbacks don't define you. They let you set new goals.

— Me

"Thank you all for coming out tonight. I think you're going to learn a lot. That's a good thing when you have a room full of educators, isn't it?"

There were chuckles in the audience at my father's joke. He was at the mic at the front of the field house in Grosse Pointe Academy, a historic brick private school on Lake Shore Drive. It was April 23, 2007. I'll always remember the date because of what happened that night.

Folding chairs lined the shiny wooden floor. Mom and I were in the front row, saving a seat for Dad. The big clock on the wall said 6:29 p.m. People were still coming in, chatting as they sat down. Mom later told me about 120 people were there.

I looked around. I saw a lot of adults I recognized. Teachers from University Liggett School. Learning specialists. People who had participated in my IEP evaluations. Parents of kids I knew. My grandparents.

On the right side of the field house, about four or five rows back, was a lady I would learn later was the superintendent of the entire Grosse Pointe Public School System (GPPSS): Dr. Suzanne Klein. That meant she had responsibility for nine elementary schools, three middle schools, two high schools, and all their students, teachers, and staff. There also were representatives in the audience of other schools in the area, like St. Paul Catholic School and Star of the Sea.

Wow. I was a little nervous, but I also really, really wanted people to catch on to how amazing the F.A.S.T. reading system was, so that other kids could get help.

"Let's get started, shall we?" Dad said. His voice echoed against the cinderblock walls and the audience got quiet.

"Many of you know that for a long time my wife, Kristine, and I have searched for a way to help our son, JT, learn to read. Tonight, we'd like to introduce you to the man who developed a system that has transformed JT's life, and we believe, can help any child who has trouble reading or writing. Stephan Tattum."

Everyone clapped politely as Steve stepped to the mic. Dad sat down next to me, smiled, and gave my shoulder a squeeze.

Looking back now, I think it was brave for my folks to organize this public demonstration. My family was well known in "the Pointes"—Grosse Pointe, Grosse Pointe Shores, Grosse Pointe Farms, Grosse Pointe Woods, and Grosse Pointe Park. And most people in the educational community knew about Mom and Dad's persistent refusal to accept what the experts—some of whom were in the audience that night—said was reality. Which was that I was illiterate for life and just had to learn to cope.

I heard Steve's voice. "JT, I'd like you to come up here and join me."

I glanced at Mom and then walked up to Steve, who wasn't wearing his normal Colorado-style shirt and jeans. He actually had on a sports jacket—something

Mom had told him he needed to wear at this sort of event in Michigan. Especially in Grosse Pointe. ("GPA is a blue-blazer type of place, Steve," she said, laughing.)

Steve took a few minutes to describe the F.A.S.T. system,[1] an integration of many techniques, how he created it, and how it worked. Then he turned to me.

"Let's show people how much you've learned, okay?"

• • •

Dr. Klein later said she was struck by the fact that an 11-year-old boy was willing to share his struggles in front of a room full of mostly adult strangers.

"I was moved by JT's earnestness and sincerity. And by the fact that he described his motive for sharing as wanting to help other kids," she said. "It was clear that

JT and his family just wanted to share what worked for them. It wasn't a marketing pitch," she said.

She also said she appreciated that the atmosphere of the meeting was positive and caring. Not blaming or negative. In fact, she remembers agreeing when Steve said that, "as teachers, we just keep trying to find a way to help kids."

● ● ●

Steve put me through a full lesson, using the magnetic white board and challenging me with multi-syllable words and nonsense phrases. It was just like what we did every morning in the F.A.S.T. House back in Denver.

Then he opened one of his books, *French Quarter Phantom*, which he wrote for middle third- and beginning fourth-grade reading levels. With him next to me, I read for about 10 minutes to the group.

"He could've read something on a much higher level," Steve explained later. "But I was certain he would be comfortable with *French Quarter Phantom*."

After we stopped, Steve told the audience we would take questions and then wind up the meeting. A few people raised their hands, and then everyone began to chat among themselves a little. It felt like the meeting was over.

Then a woman approached us. I recognized her as someone who had worked with me when I was younger.

"I'm sorry," she said, sounding a little sad. "But I find it so hard to believe that JT can read like this. I worked with him. I know where he was as a reader just months ago."

I looked at my parents. Mom looked stunned. The woman seemed to be implying that Steve, my folks, and I were putting on a giant act, that we were trying to deceive people. Why in the world would we do that?

Steve calmly asked the woman, "Is there a piece of paper or something in your purse that has writing on it?"

She picked up her bag and rummaged around in it, finding a sales receipt.

"Bring it here," Steve said. I sat still.

The woman handed the paper to Steve, who glanced at it and then gave it to me. "Read it," he said.

I looked down, squinting, because the type was tiny. "Fresh Farms Market ... " I began. "Cheddar cheese ..."

I glanced up. The woman was smiling. She had tears in her eyes.

● ● ●

A month later my semester at Denver Academy ended. The four weeks since returning from the quick trip to Michigan for the presentation had whizzed by. I didn't know what would come out of that meeting, but I was all the more certain that F.A.S.T. could help a lot of kids.

After all, I was proof. I had come to Denver barely reading at the kindergarten level and hardly writing at all. Now, five months later, although I wasn't up to fifth-grade speed, in vocabulary and comprehension I was a fifth-grade reader.

Mrs. Friend was there to say goodbye, and Steve. It was a beautiful day. I was glad to be going home, but I also felt really sad. I started to cry a little.

"J, you don't need to cry," my dad said. He and Mom were anxious to get to the airport. "You'll see everyone again when you come back in the fall."

"Dad, I'm not crying because I'm going to missing these guys." I shook my head. I suddenly realized what was wrong. "I'm crying for all the kids back in Michigan who can't move to Denver and learn to read."

Everyone was silent for a moment.

Then Steve said, "Get tutors and teachers together. I'll come to Michigan to train them."

Chapter 22

BIG GOALS

I can't change the direction of the wind, but I can adjust my sails and always reach my destination.

— Jimmy Dean

My seven Boll cousins took their seats in chairs around the long, shiny conference table. Some sat next to their parents, my aunts, and uncles. Through the big windows behind where Mom and Dad were sitting, I could see the June sunlight bouncing off the boats bobbing in the harbor at the Grosse Pointe Yacht Club on Lake St. Clair. I loved this place.

Papi, wearing a dark blue suit, looked like a ship's captain, which was appropriate since we were in what the club called the Commodore's Room. Nani was next to him, sparkling in a gold and white dress.

For as long as I could remember, my Boll grandparents would ask us grandchildren to set goals for our upcoming year. They'd also ask us to report on how well we met last year's goals. Sometimes Papi and Nani would take a grandson or daughter out for lunch and talk one-on-one with them. Oftentimes, we'd all be expected to dress nicely and attend an annual family meeting.

Papi and Nani loved us and wanted to support our dreams—sometimes with advice and accountability and prayer, sometimes financially. Especially when it came to education. My grandparents had built a very successful business from the ground up—literally—and had not been able to go to college. That made them want to promote and support education whenever they could.

I was third to the youngest of the eight grandkids. My mom's brother, John, and his wife, Donna, were parents of Amanda, Alex, Abigail, and Anton. My mom's sister, Lora, and her husband, Sergio, had Justin, Jaco, and Casey.

I had never shared my educational achievements before. This year—after meeting Steve Tattum and finishing fifth grade at Denver Academy—it was going to be different!

"So, kids, what have you been proud of this year?" Papi asked.

I was sitting next to him on his right side. My hand shot up. Papi turned toward me and smiled. I felt a surge of excitement and stood.

"One of my goals this year"—I could feel the big grin on my face—"was to learn to read. And I did!"

For a moment no one said anything. I glanced around. Some looked pretty confused. Then it hit me. They hadn't known I *couldn't* read.

"What?!"

I don't remember which cousin blurted that out. I looked at Mom and Dad. I hadn't told them I was going to make my little announcement, so they were surprised too, but they were smiling.

"Tell 'em, J," Dad said.

I took a deep breath.

"Well, you all know I went to a new school this winter and spring in Denver, right?" I went on to share about struggling academically since preschool, about being told I was going to be illiterate all my life, about meeting

Steve, and about his amazing reading program and Denver Academy.

"When I started there I could barely make out words most kindergarteners know. Now, I can read at a fifth-grade level!"

"JT, honey, that's wonderful!" Nani said with a big smile. My cousins gave me high-fives, and said encouraging things too. That made me feel good.

Papi was quiet. Later he said he was feeling a little embarrassed. "I hadn't realized JT couldn't read at all," he said. "I didn't want to admit to the grandchildren that I didn't know. The truth of the matter is, all the cousins thought he could read."

It wasn't like Mom and Dad had wanted to keep anything a secret. It was just that they always tried to be positive and to not worry people.

Everyone in the family realized that since birth I had faced life-threatening medical issues and major surgeries. But, the hospitalizations and procedures were so frequent that whenever I had to have another one, the reaction among my cousins was like, "Oh, JT's in the hospital again."

When it came to school, they knew I was challenged. But they didn't know how severely.

After my announcement, we kids continued going around the table sharing accomplishments and goals. In addition to improving at reading, writing, and arithmetic, I shared how I planned to get my golf-cart license for Ocean Reef, where my grandparents spend winters, and my hunting safety license.

Somewhere I heard about having a "bucket list." Problem was, with my short-term memory loss, I kept thinking of cool things to do and forgetting to write them down! It wasn't until I was in college that I got the idea to put them on my smart phone! (I've checked off a few now, but am looking forward to do a lot more!)

BUCKET LIST

- ☐ Go helicopter skiing
- ☐ Go skydiving
- ☑ Be published
- ☐ Swim with a whale shark
- ☐ Swim with a great white shark
- ☑ Learn to SCUBA dive
- ☐ Drive across the United States
- ☐ Visit the Arctic and Antarctic
- ☐ Hike the Triple Crown (Appalachian, Continental Divide, Pacific Crest trails)
- ☐ Ski the Alps
- ☐ Ski Japan
- ☑ Hike Mount Kilimanjaro
- ☑ Drive the Autobahn
- ☐ Climb all 14er's in Colorado
- ☑ Learn how to kiteboard
- ☐ Climb to the base camp of Mount Everest
- ☑ Write a memoir of my life
- ☑ Establish a foundation
- ☐ Get a pilot's license
- ☐ Learn to surf
- ☑ Earn a 100-ton captain's license
- ☑ Get a CPL license
- ☐ Go transatlantic sailing
- ☐ Run a marathon

What I hadn't shared, though, was my biggest goal—and one I know my parents were also committed to, too: spreading the word about Steve's reading program so that other kids who were like me could learn to read, too.

● ● ●

Remember that big book I lugged home from school that I couldn't read? A year later Steve surprised me with a gift to honor a year of reading. "Here, here's a very big book that you can read now!" he said.

I unwrapped the present to find *The Invention of Hugo Cabret*, by Brian Selznick. It was a good three inches thick! I haven't made it all the way through yet, but I plan to keep at it.

Steve had a waiting list in Denver for specialized instruction and teacher training. He didn't need Michigan. But he had promised. Mom and Dad started talking, emailing, and sending info to as many influential people as they could think of, to drum up interest and set up presentations.

All sorts of things were happening behind the scenes. After the April presentation at Grosse Pointe Academy, GPPSS Superintendent Suzanne Klein said she and her colleagues left the meeting curious. "We decided we needed to learn more about this system."

Dr. Klein called together the district's head of the reading support department, all reading specialists, and the assistant superintendent.

"We all agreed we needed to find out more," she said. They learned that Steve was going to hold F.A.S.T. training workshops at GPA, so Mrs. Klein sent her reading specialists. Grosse Pointe Foundation for Public Education (GPFPE) helped cover the cost.

The positive outcome motivated Dr. Klein to move the district from a decentralized approach toward reading intervention to a district-wide, centralized model, she said. All reading specialists would use F.A.S.T. in their sessions. Some or all the district's first-grade teachers would be trained as well, to introduce the reading program in their regular curriculum. Dr. Klein recognized that F.A.S.T. also helped children who weren't identified as problem readers.

There also was a parent component. The district arranged for parent workshops with Steve, introducing them to F.A.S.T. and showing them ways they could accelerate at home what their kids were learning in class.

Lisa Vreede, who was on the Grosse Pointe Public School Board of Education at the time, became a strong supporter of F.A.S.T. and attended some of the training sessions. She later became the assistant director and then an advisory board member of the GPFPE, which works to augment the programs of Grosse Pointe Public School System.[1]

By 2008, all GPPSS specialists were trained. By 2013, F.A.S.T. had been used with 1,300 children. The starting point was in second grade. All nine elementary schools used F.A.S.T., with pretty impressive results.[2] The foundation had donated $250,000.

In fact, more than three quarters of everyone at that first presentation Steve and I gave went on to get F.A.S.T. training. For years, Steve was invited to come back on a monthly basis, and even now—a dozen years later—he regularly visits Michigan to hold training sessions.

I appeared at almost every presentation until I went off to college. I shared my story, demonstrated my progress, and took questions from the teachers. Here was a common one: What advice did I have for teachers to help them reach kids like me?

(I always had an answer for that one! Don't always call on us last! If teachers would at least change up the order, then it wouldn't feel so stigmatizing.)

Steve now estimates that he has trained 1,500 teachers throughout Michigan, helping who knows how many children. And here's the thing: all of these changed lives would not have happened if the door to attending

University Liggett for Middle School hadn't been slammed shut.

Sometimes tough experiences lead to terrific outcomes. You just have to keep yourself moving forward and trust God will open a window.

Now we had to figure what I was going to do for sixth grade.

Chapter 23

NAVIGATING THE MIDDLE YEARS

If you are not willing to risk the unusual, you will have to settle for the ordinary.
— Jim Rohn

"Uh oh."

Captain John Roberts was frowning. It's never good when the captain of a boat you're cruising on in thick fog says "Uh oh." Especially one as calm and experienced as John.

I glanced up at him. It was very early on a morning in 2007, the summer after Denver Academy. John and I hadn't been gone from the Grosse Pointe Yacht Club for more than a few minutes.

Dawn had broken clear. Then a band of low clouds had rolled in over the water, reducing visibility to no more than 10 feet.

"The radar's out."

John was a hired captain who had become a family friend. We were taking *The Jester*, my folks' 63-foot sport fishing boat, from Grosse Pointe Shores to Bay Harbor in Northern Michigan so that it would be ready for our family's summer vacation. We often would spend a few weeks exploring the region and Canada's North Channel, one of the best freshwater cruising grounds in the world. We'd meet up with other boating families we knew from the yacht club. It was a wonderful time of fun and reconnecting.

John's and my route meant we had to cross Lake St. Clair north to the mouth of St. Clair River. We'd cruise up the 40-mile long waterway that flows between the United States and Canada. Then we would spill out onto Lake Huron—the second largest Great Lake and the fifth largest fresh-water lake on the planet—and point north for 200 or so miles.

We next would turn west through the Straits of Mackinac at the top of Michigan's "mitt" shape. Then we would empty into Lake Michigan, turn south a bit, stop for fuel in Petoskey, and dock in nearby Bay Harbor.

That was the plan, anyway. I had been looking forward to the cruise for weeks. But, without radar, we'd have to slow to eight or 10 knots. The one-day, 10-hour trip would take two days, and with this fog, everything would be a bit more nerve-wracking.

With John, though, I had learned to stay calm and look for solutions. He swears he never actually taught me that, but I picked it up early just by observing him.

I stared out into the fog. I was just a kid; what could I do?

Then an idea popped into my head. It helped that I had grown up on boats and loved everything about them and the water, just as my dad did. I dropped to my knees and tucked my head under the dashboard. At 11, I was still small enough. I was able to read a tiny green menu on the radar screen, and figure out that I could switch some cables and restart the program.

"JT! What did you do? The radar is back up!" John said.

I grinned. It felt so good to be able to use my new reading skills to accomplish something important.

• • •

The summer was full of fun, whether boating with the family up to the Old Club on Harsen's Island or Northern Michigan, hanging out with Andrew, or doing water sports like Jet Skis or wake-boarding with Gregory, Thomas ("T.J."), Kyle, C.J., William, Bobby, Andy, and the gang.

But, every day was also full of work! I had so much to catch up on! Whenever Steve visited Michigan to train teachers I had sessions with him, and helped out with his demonstrations. I also met with F.A.S.T. tutors, including my former first-grade teacher, Mrs. Peggy Dettlinger, who had accepted an invitation from my mom to work with me before the school year started again in the fall.[1]

Retraining my brain was hard work! And sometimes there were hurdles. Here's a small, but funny example of one.

One day I was working with Steve. We had done the F.A.S.T. phonics board and now we were reading. I was not bored at all, or lacking sleep. But, I couldn't help myself—I kept yawning.

Steve remembers the scene. "He's yawning regularly. I walk over to the coffee machine and get some coffee. I glance at JT and he's no longer yawning. Then, as I'm walking back to him, suddenly he starts yawning," Steve recalls. "I turn around and go the other direction. JT stops yawning."

Another teacher, Wendy, was in the workroom too. Steve asked Wendy to walk over to me. As she did, I didn't yawn. Of course, I was clueless. It was absolutely unconscious. Then Steve came back, and I started to yawn again.

What was that all about?

What Steve figured out was, I had developed a conditioned response for yawning around Steve, because our work—without me being aware of it—was exhausting. Why? Because my brain was spending a bunch of energy growing dendrites.

"Actually, we know that people grow connections between neurons when learning to read, and that's exhausting. Neurons that fire together, wire together and that's what was happening to JT," Steve says. "He was associating me with exhaustion, and I became a conditioned response for yawning—whether or not he was reading."

Steve demonstrated the whole thing to my mom. "I don't care how much he yawns," she said. "You're still going to work with him."

● ● ●

Mom and Dad had talked with me about returning to the Denver Academy that fall. I loved Colorado and liked the school. But boy, I really loved being home. I didn't know what to do.

One day Mom was at a sidewalk sale at Pointe Pedlar, a kitchen store that used to be in The Village section of downtown Grosse Pointe. She bumped into Mrs. Donna Martin, a family friend. Mrs. Martin had just retired from full-time teaching and was working at the store while substitute-teaching and praying about what she should do next.

Something clicked in Mom's mind. She went to talk with Dad. He liked her idea.

What, Mom and Dad asked, about setting up a homeschool for a while instead of me attending traditional school? What about asking Mrs. Martin if she would be willing to train in F.A.S.T. and be my home-school teacher?

There was only one hesitancy. As I've said, education is really important to my parents and to both sets of grandparents. Pa, my dad's father, had been a school principal for 30 years. My Aunt Cathy was a teacher. Would there be some push-back on the plan?

Mrs. Martin actually went to talk with Pa, as she was determined that the curriculum we used should be a good one and be current with what the area school districts were teaching. That way I would be ready to return to a traditional school, if and when that happened.

Eventually Pa and Ma, Papi and Nani, and the rest of the family saw the benefits to the homeschool. It allowed me to pour everything I could into getting stronger as a reader and writer.

● ● ●

My folks transformed the extra rooms in our carriage house above the garage into two classrooms. Mrs. Martin and I met there, every weekday, from 8:30 a.m. to 12:30 p.m. *For three years!*

Mrs. Martin ran our homeschool like a traditional classroom, except with a lot more flexibility and creativity. I dressed in school clothes each day. (No hanging out in pajamas!)

One room was set up as a work space and computer and science room. The other had a bookcase, whiteboard, and a U-shaped desk. Every morning we did two or so hours of F.A.S.T. with lots of drills and memorization. Mrs. Martin encouraged art, and she also read novels to me during breaks. On Fridays we cooked! The carriage house had a kitchen in which was used science and math to create a meal. Sometimes we'd invite guests, like my grandparents, Uncle Gene, Aunt Diena, Uncle Ed, Aunt Rieni, and Fritz and Anne Rector. That was fun!

"My first goal was to build up your confidence, both personally and in reading and writing," Mrs. Martin told me later. "In sixth grade you were pretty shy."

She understood that I learn best by hearing, seeing, and applying concepts. We studied videos. Once Mrs. Martin created a scavenger hunt in Detroit. I had to read the clues and strategize how to discover everything on the list.

We went to the library. We took many field trips, from going to the grocery store to touring the Henry Ford Museum and the Ford Rouge Factory, and visiting Selfridge Air National Guard Base.

In eighth grade we did "job-shadowing," where I spent a chunk of time with a professional, like an attorney, a police officer, an ER doctor, a heart surgeon, just to name a few. I decided none of those professions were for me, but it was fun to learn about them.

● ● ●

I practiced with the lacrosse team at Grosse Pointe Academy, until my doctors put a stop to me, as a tethered-cord patient, playing contact sports. But, it was crucial that I regularly work out, do stretches, and build my core strength for the same reason. It was more than just being a middle-school kid who needed to get out of the classroom and burn off energy. (Okay, it was also nice to get out of the classroom.)

So, my folks arranged to have a physical trainer named P.J. Vlahantones come to the house three times a week. P.J. was not just a physical trainer; he became a friend and a mentor.

He made our hour together fun and taught me a lot about being an athlete. He and I would jog, ride bikes, and lift weights. In one of his epic challenges, he had me do lunges all the way from our driveway down the road about three-quarters of a mile and back!

● ● ●

Not everyone who struggles in school can hire a private teacher and learn at home. The point is to look for creative options. Whether your boat's radar gives out or your brain gets tired, I discovered that the best response is to stay calm and never give up.

There was another advantage to doing grades six to eight at home that I didn't hear about until I became an adult.

"Middle school can be a tough time for kids—socially, spiritually, morally," says Mom. "To not have JT be in the middle of the typical stuff—you know, all that goes into trying to fit in—we think that was a good thing. By allowing JT to be homeschooled, God provided him the opportunity to focus on what mattered for his education."

Turns out that it would be a blessing to not be following a conventional school day. Within months I would be facing more medical challenges that would alter everything.

Chapter 24

NO BAD DAYS—JUST HARD ONES

Peace begins with a smile.

— Mother Teresa

There's a little tube-like tail at the bottom of your large intestine where it bends and connects to your small intestine. It looks like an earth worm. It's the appendix.

Scientists aren't sure about the purpose of the appendix.[1] One theory is that it's a storehouse for good bacteria that fights infections and helps the digestive system recover after illnesses. (Or, maybe, jokes Dr. Peña, it was created just to give surgeons lots of income taking care of appendicitis!)

I know the purpose of *my* appendix. And you'll never guess it.

● ● ●

Because of all my chronic VATER-caused problems, I spent most of my childhood being hooked up one way or another to a catheter once a day for an enema. Most of the time my parents or a trusted babysitter or medical people inserted the tube and hooked up the liquid laxatives that would flush out my colon. (Fun topic, I know.) It was awkward and unpleasant.

And when I was older and had to do it myself? *Really* awkward and unpleasant. The last time I was at SpringHill Camp and had to give myself my treatment, I had to hang the IV bag filled with solution on the door handle of the boys' restroom to get enough gravity for it to flow. Then, like at home, I had to lie on the floor for an hour. At camp, though, it was cold tile because I hadn't thought to put down a towel like Mom did at home.

So, in 2008, when Mom and Dad told me of a procedure Dr. Peña could do that would improve things, I was excited. Maybe it would mean more privacy and more freedom. Maybe I could go places and not have to worry about how I was going to do a treatment.

By age 13 I was old enough and healthy enough to be considered for a Malone procedure. It would change my life!

● ● ●

So, on October 26, 2008, I was back at familiar Cincinnati Children's Hospital Medical Center.

Dad, Mom, and I had taken off from Detroit early that day. By 10:30 a.m., Ohio time, I was admitted. By 1 p.m., the nurses had an NG tube in my nose and GoLightly (a laxative with which I was very familiar) was flowing. It was going to be a busy day going back and forth to the bathroom to get completely cleaned out before surgery the next day.

That night I spent my very first night alone in a hospital room. I had said goodnight to my parents around midnight as they left for their hotel—the old Vernon Manor. I didn't mind being alone.

When Mom and Dad came back the next day, I was IV'd and prepped for surgery. Dr. Peña made one last visit to pre-op before I was wheeled into the operating room. Mom and Dad looked on.

"JT, do you understand what I am going to do today?" he asked in his distinctive accent. Even though he had lived in the United States for decades, you could still hear his native Mexico in his voice.

I understand now what the operation was. But, back then it was a little hard to follow.

Remember me mentioning the appendix? Well, the surgery is called an appendicostomy, which was rather new at that point. It's also known as a Malone antegrade continence enema (MACE or Malone ACE) procedure, or just Malone for short. (It was named after the surgeon, Dr. Patrick Malone, who popularized it in the 1990s.)[2]

What did solving my need for daily enemas have to do with an appendix? Well, it's pretty amazing.

During the appendicostomy the surgeon makes a very small opening in the abdomen, hunts for the appendix, opens its tip to form a passageway into the bowels, and then connects it to the abdominal wall, usually at the umbilicus (the belly button or navel). The surgeon makes a tiny hole—no one would know it's there—and creates a one-way valve using existing tissue. (You don't want the poop to seep out!)

The valve becomes the port for the tube through which the enema solution could flow, cleaning out the patient's insides.

So, if it worked, the procedure was going to become my ON button to freedom.

The only question was, did I even have an appendix?

● ● ●

Believe it or not, some people are born without an appendix. Some who have a lot of surgeries (like me) can lose them during procedures. If I didn't have one, Dr. Peña was going to have to create one!

That additional work would add hours to the operation. He most likely wouldn't have time for a few other tasks he was going to try to do, like fixing a lumpy old scar in my stomach. (I had asked Dad to request that Dr. Peña straighten it out, if possible.)

So, for a few hours, my folks just sat and waited, praying for the best. Then at 2:40 p.m. a message came from the O.R.: They found an appendix!

At 4:15 p.m. Dr. Peña was done and I was in post-op. He summoned Dad and Mom for an update. He was very happy. Everything had gone well! *Thank you, Lord.*

My folks visited me in my room. I had a slight fever, which was expected, and some swelling and pain. Mom's cool hand stroked my forehead.

"You're going to have a couple of bad days," she said.

"No, Mom," I replied. I knew it was all worth it. "There are no bad days, only hard days!"

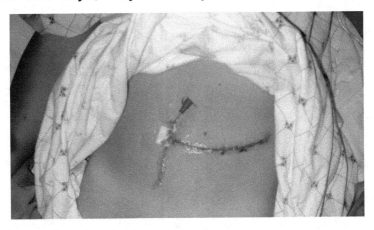

● ● ●

There were many hard days after the Malone operation. As my incision healed I got used to catheterizing myself though my belly button. But of course, nothing ever turns out simply when it comes to my body.

The bathroom visits were much more frequent and unpleasant than expected. One week in February 2009 I logged 15 to 18 trips a day. Not good. This was one reason, among many, that I was thankful I was being homeschooled!

I didn't let the bathroom calls stop me from skiing with Ladi and the family during our spring vacation in Colorado. But, the difficulties were disappointing, and puzzling.

Then it got harder and harder to get the tube through the valve. I'd try to the point of tears. Dad would try, Mom would try. Everyone was frustrated. Finally, the opening just closed up.

We flew back to Cincinnati. Dr. Peña couldn't get the catheter in either. So, he got out some dilators. It wasn't fun, but after an hour or so of working on my belly button, he got the smallest dilator in the valve, and worked up to a size 8 catheter. He left that in and taped it. I was to keep it there for two weeks.

Then I had to come back for another operation, to enlarge the hole in the belly button. According to Dr.

Peña, a "narrowing of the Malone orifice" only happens to 10 percent of his patients.

Aren't I special!

• • •

Mom was saying good-night to me one night in April soon after the second surgery. This valve was working great, but I was sore and tired. She looked sad.

"I'm so sorry you had to endure this pain today, JT. I'm so sorry you have to go through everything you have to go through, every day."

I know all that I have had to experience since birth has been hard on my parents. They have always been amazing models for me of Christ. They have taught me that the love of God gives us hope. This world is not our permanent home and our troubles on earth are temporary.

Dr. Peña had told me that he wanted to give me what he called a "better quality of life," and I'm so grateful he did. Things weren't perfect, but now I could plan. I could expect my body to generally follow a schedule. I could go places. I could hang out with friends. I could envision attending high school, and maybe even college. Maybe do even bigger things.

"It's okay, Mom," I said. "When we have our heavenly bodies, we'll be all healed and perfect. This is just the way it is for now."

All I had to do was to have faith and keep going.

Chapter 25

A LEAP OF FAITH

Believe you can and you're halfway there.

— Theodore Roosevelt

I'm standing on a platform sticking out from the Victoria Falls Bridge near the Victoria Falls, the largest waterfall in the world. I barely hear the hum of spectators behind me above the roar of the Zambezi River 111 meters, or 364 feet, below us—twice the height of North America's Niagara Falls.[1] My heart is pounding.

A harness crisscrosses my chest and encircles my thighs. My ankles are wrapped tight with wide straps on top of a thick yellow pad. They're hooked to a large elastic cord that lies next to me like a coiled snake. I can hardly breathe.

I stretch out my arms like wings and focus downriver as far as I can see. I can feel the jumpmaster's hand in the middle of my back. The wind and spray swirl up from below and pummel my face.

The man tells me he is going to count to three. I force myself to take a deep breath.

"One . . ."

"Two . . ."

He pushes me off the bridge.

● ● ●

I had finished up eighth grade with Mrs. Martin that June of 2010. Before our family trip to Africa in late July, my parents had told me they wanted me to return to a traditional school in September to start ninth grade. The Mestdagh homeschool—which we nicknamed the U of M, for the "University of Mestdagh"—was officially closed!

I didn't want to say goodbye to Mrs. Martin, with whom I had spent every school day for three years! She understood how my brain worked and all the challenges I had to overcome, and she made learning fun. I would miss her.

But, I was 14.5 now and I knew it would be good for me to figure out how to learn in a classroom among peers. Mom and Dad said I could choose between the local public high school, Grosse Pointe South (known as just "South"), or University Liggett. I hadn't decided which yet.

One man wanted to influence the decision: Liggett's new head of school, Dr. Joe Healey. The other headmaster, thankfully, was gone. Dad, as a member of Liggett's board of trustees, had met Dr. Healey before he was hired, and had liked him. Mom did, too.

Dr. Healey doesn't remember this, but as Mom recalls it, he unexpectedly came knocking on our front door while I was still being home-schooled, I guess to talk with my parents about enrolling me.

And it's funny to hear that this distinguished man—with his European education, advanced degrees and decades as a teacher, scholar, and headmaster at prestigious schools—teasingly told Mom and Dad that even if it meant that he might end up on the front of the *Grosse Pointe News*, he would stand in front of South and bar the doors to prevent me from going there.

"No aspersions toward South," he would later explain, smiling. "But they were large, and although they had a special education program, they had too many kids to tailor something to JT's needs."

That Liggett might be able to tailor something for my educational needs was a new idea to us, though. Would returning there turn out as heart-breaking as when I was kicked out in fifth grade? Should I take that leap of faith?

● ● ●

I wasn't thinking of school that day on the bridge in Zimbabwe in southern Africa, though. Nor was I thinking of what was happening in my elimination system.

Children who undergo the Malone procedure from that point on typically must use 500 cc's of sodium chloride in their daily treatment. Because of transportation security rules, we could not travel with this liquid. So, mine had to be shipped to Africa during our family's three-week trip there. We actually prayed that it would arrive—using it was the *only* way I could get rid of toxins and keep healthy.

But, because nothing ever seems to go as planned when it comes to my body, for some unknown reason I actually started to absorb the sodium from the solution. My fingers and toes got puffy from water retention, and my eyes swelled up!

(When I returned stateside, Dr. Peña had me try different combinations of substances, and eventually we settled on water, glycerin, and Dr. Bonner's Soap. That's what I use to this day.)

• • •

The mist from Victoria Falls, one of the modern-day Seven Natural Wonders of the World, rises more than 1,300 feet and can be seen from a distance of 30 miles. The sound of the falls can be heard almost as far: 25 miles away. No wonder its local name is *Mosi-oa-Tunya*, which means "the smoke that thunders."

We were traveling with neighbors from home, the Fruehaufs, and some of their children and grandchildren. The trip was a celebration of Mr. Fruehauf turning 80. Our rooms were in the beautiful Victoria Falls Hotel—nicknamed the Grand Lady. It was built in 1904 during British colonial rule of Northern Rhodesia (now Zambia) and Southern Rhodesia (now Zimbabwe). The Zambezi River is the border between Zimbabwe and Zambia.

A few of the adults and some of the older kids got the idea of doing the bungee jump. When they asked if I wanted to jump too, I didn't hesitate. Of course!

I went to ask my parents. To my surprise, Dad said yes. I went back to the group excited. Later I learned that Mom had grabbed his arm and looked at him "like he had three eyeballs."

"Jim, are you kidding me? What about his back!? He's had tethered cord surgery . . . !"

Dad replied, "Don't worry—JT is too young and small. They won't let him do it and then we won't be the one saying no."

I indeed was smaller than the published minimum weight (40 kg, or about 88 pounds). But, Dad forgot that rules aren't always followed in Africa.

To Mom's horror, she watches as the entire group of us are registered. The jump operators wave me through, and we line up to get fitted with our harnesses. She looks at Dad, like "Do something!"

But, before they can, it is my turn.

I am tethered to the bridge and bouncing like a rubber band in 364 feet of air.

What I remember as I dive into that amazing long free fall is the adrenaline rush and feeling my stomach in my throat and hearing the rush of air in my ears and watching the river get closer and closer and closer. Then *boing!* I'm shooting up again. Like the effect when the surgeon severed my spinal cord when I was 10 and said it snapped like a rubber band.

The force of the bounce spins me and now my face is skyward and I can see the bridge dark against the bright light and I can tell I'm grinning.

This. Is. So. Fun!

Then down again! Falling, down down down to the river, where the cord catches me and shoots me up and down again two more times. Finally, I'm bouncing at the bottom now, like the little ball in the paddle ball game. Then I'm swinging in the wind, head down. It's been maybe a minute since I jumped. But, it feels like forever!

Over the roar of the water I start to hear the far-away sound of a man singing an African song. The singing comes closer and closer.

There is a crew of men whose job it is to belay off a lower level of the bridge and retrieve jumpers. Suddenly someone is hanging in the air alongside me. He smiles and hooks our harnesses together. Then he spins me upside down, or rather, right side up. Now I realize how much blood had collected in my head.

We are hauled up to an underneath platform, where people grab me. I'm lightheaded and wobbly, but euphoric as they plant my feet on solid metal. Boy, does that feel good!

• • •

One morning, a year and a half later, my parents were watching the "Today" show, when they heard a teaser about a young woman bungee-jumping off the Victoria Falls Bridge. They were excited to watch the report—until they learned what had actually happened.

The woman, a 22-year-old Australian, experienced every jumper's—and every jumper's parents'—nightmare.

Her bungee cord broke. She plummeted into the river below.

Luckily, it had rained the day before and the river was full. Luckily, she had landed in water rather than on the rocks along the shore. Luckily, there were no crocodiles nearby. Although bruised from head to foot, with a collapsed lung and a broken collarbone, she lived to tell the tale.

"Thank God she survived!" Mom said. "It is unbelievable she did. God was watching over her."

The story reminded my folks (and me, when they told me about it) that none of us are in control of our own lives. Ultimately, only God is. They thought back to our time in Africa and their attempt at protecting me. As much as they had always looked out for me since the day I was born, they had to trust that my life was in God's hands.

They had raised me to jump into life in faith and be wise, but brave. They had to be brave, too. Believing that God is infinitely loving and all-knowing and has a purpose for every single child He created, Mom and Dad had to trust and let go.

It was a lesson we'd practice countless times in the next four years.

Chapter 26

THE TEST PILOT

A negative mind will never give you a positive life.

— Anonymous

When I saw the sign for the conference room I stopped and took a deep breath.

I was back at University Liggett School—four years after being kicked out. Now, I was going to meet my ninth-grade teachers and try to convince them that not only could I learn, I could also keep up with the school's top-level academics.

It was late August, a week or so before the start of classes. After Africa, my folks and I had decided to give Liggett a try. Or, maybe that should be, to let Liggett give me a try. There was a new administration, a new philosophy of education, even a new student support services department. We had new hope.

But, neither side knew what we were getting into!

I wiped my palms on my new khaki pants and opened the door.

The room wasn't huge. Around the rectangular table were half a dozen adults. Some were standing, some seated. I recognized one lady.

Beth Beckmann turned and smiled. She was the Associate Head of School and Dean of Faculty. She was the one who had talked with my parents about having this meeting—and having me attend by myself. "Hello, Mrs. Beckmann," I said.

"JT, we're glad you're here," she said, shaking my hand. "Now, let me introduce you to everyone."

Because it's hard for me to remember names at first, I wasn't able to catch all that Mrs. Beckmann said. Later, I would put names to faces. One woman was Liggett's school psychologist in charge of student support services. One was a brand-new learning specialist. The remaining people were the English, history, math, and science teachers whose courses Mrs. Beckmann had signed me up for.

"JT, why don't you tell us about your story? What have been your experiences with school and learning?" Mrs. Beckmann said.

So, I started sharing. I described not being able to learn to read or write during the lower grades and how we discovered that I had very, very bad dyslexia and a weak

206

short-term memory. I mentioned getting a bunch of tests and trying out well-known reading programs that didn't help.

Then I told how my folks discovered Stephan Tattum and his amazing F.A.S.T. program, known outside Michigan as Tattum Reading. I said I moved to the Denver Academy for five months, where I got daily F.A.S.T. tutoring and was in a classroom that used unique ways of teaching designed for kids with learning differences.

Lastly, I caught them up on three years being home-schooled by a wonderful professional teacher also trained in F.A.S.T. Then I summarized what my strengths were, what my weaknesses were, and what my needs (as far as education) were.

When I stopped talking, the room was silent.

● ● ●

"Liggett wasn't set up to deal with different learners," Mrs. Beckmann recalled later.

Before coming to Grosse Pointe, Mrs. Beckmann had worked with Dr. Healey for many years in a prestigious private school in New York City, and had been an administrator at many other independent schools too. She knew all about them. When it came to not dealing well with kids with learning differences, Liggett was like most schools back then. Curriculum was designed for the majority of kids, and in Liggett's case, most of the kids were high achievers.

If you were different, you didn't fit in.

"In formal education," Dr. Healey told an acquaintance later, "the set-up is one of 'sorting' kids—measuring them according to tests to put them into boxes. It's all based on numbers, on data. Not on potential or passion."

Sometimes kids might break out of the box, such as through sports or the arts and theatre. But mostly the process meant only certain kids could succeed. "It doesn't take emotional intelligence into account, for instance," Dr. Healey said. In the traditional system, "there is one path to success. If you're not on it, you won't succeed."

When Dr. Healey came to Liggett, he set out to create multiple paths to success. To help in that, he launched the student support services department, led by Dr. Michelle Ondersma, a licensed clinical psychologist.

Then, when Dr. Healey learned that my parents wanted me to return to a traditional school, he told Mrs. Beckmann that "it has to be here, and we have to make this work."

No one knew just how, though.

Of course, I didn't know any of this. I was just an undersized freshman starting high school, which was nerve-wracking enough.

● ● ●

After I left the meeting, Mrs. Beckmann turned to the group and asked, "What do you think?"

The overall reaction, she said, was uncertainty and a little fear. These were fine teachers. But, they had taught a specific way for years—some for decades. They didn't know what was going to be needed, they didn't know anything about "accommodations," and they didn't know if they could be successful.

But, kindly, they all thought I might be a good test pilot for trying something new and for seeing if it would fly.

Why? "Because he knew himself so well. He knew his needs and he knew how to advocate for himself," said Mrs. Beckmann. "Many, many kids struggle with learning and come into ninth grade just figuring that out. JT was way ahead of the curve. He owned who he was as a learner."

I may have known my learning weaknesses and strengths, but now we had to make things work in a high-school classroom. I say "we" because it was going to take everyone, from Dr. Healey and the administration to the teachers and support staff down to my parents and me. And there was no blueprint.

The administrators had to reassure the teachers that they could experiment, which meant they might try something that didn't work, and that would be all right.

There was also the issue of fairness. The faculty grappled with whether doing things differently from kid to kid was "fair."

"Teachers often needed 'permission.' To hear from the administration that, 'It's okay, you don't have to treat every child exactly the same,' "said Mrs. Beckmann. "Treating a child fairly isn't treating every child the same."

● ● ●

Right before the school year began, Mrs. Beckmann arranged for a Skype call with a man she and Dr. Healey had worked with who was an expert in educational technology, Jay Trevorrow. We had a fun conversation, me in Grosse Pointe and Mr. Trevorrow on his balcony in Riverdale, New York, talking about tech ideas.

In a few months, Dr. Healey and Mrs. Beckmann had persuaded Mr. Trevorrow to leave New York and become Liggett's new director of technology. He helped the teachers integrate new tools into my learning toolkit. Things like using audio books and videos, and recording classroom presentations, and taking photos of notes on the board (because I couldn't write things down fast enough).

My English teacher, Mr. Andy Knote, worked with me a lot. Two examples of adjustments Mr. Knote made involved the weekly vocabulary quizzes and essays.

Every week we had list of 20 vocabulary words to learn. The quiz would randomly test on 10 words out of the 20. Mr. Knote decided that he'd cut my list to 10 words, and I'd be tested on five.

When it came to writing papers, the normal assignment would be an essay of 1,000 words, or roughly four pages double-spaced. Mr. Knote cut that in half for me, as well.

"JT would have taken so long to complete four pages that it would have been twice as much work as the other kids," Mr. Knote said. "He learned the same structure, though, and had to make clear points and a persuasive argument."

I would come in during free period or study hall to get feedback on material, too. I appreciated all the extra time Mr. Knote and the other teachers gave me.

It wasn't always smooth going.

Things were tough in my freshman science class. I couldn't recall all the biology terms and failed the first exam. I didn't know it at the time, but the teacher went to Dr. Healey, showed him the big F, and basically said, *I told you this wasn't going to work.*

I will always be grateful for how Dr. Healey responded. He asked that the teacher meet with me and asked me to draw what the test had been on—the inside of the cell—and describe each part.

Later Dr. Healey said the teacher had reported back. "You're absolutely right. JT knows the concept better than most of my students!"

I faced the same challenge in my sophomore year with a different teacher. I was still struggling with vocabulary, so I called Steve for advice. He and I stayed in close contact.

"JT, here is what you are going to do," said Steve. "You're going to draw a central picture about whatever word you are dealing with. Then, around that picture, you're going to use that center like mapping, and you're going to connect pictures of your other vocab words related to that central picture."

That's what I did. The next day in class, the teacher was giving us some time to study. He came by and saw me drawing.

"JT, I'm giving you time to study and here you are drawing!" he said. He hadn't caught on to the way I learned.

When I explained that this was how I studied, he looked skeptical. But, I aced the test!

The adjustments were going pretty well, and I began to feel more confident that I could handle school. Mrs. Ondersma said I had resilience. Working hard, staying positive, and trusting the good people around me helped. I know now that those are invaluable skills to have in life.

Unfortunately, my body decided again to not cooperate. It turned out that I wasn't going to make it through the school year without another major surgery.

Chapter 27

TETHERED

(AGAIN)

Success is not final, failure is not fatal: it is courage to continue that counts.

— Winston Churchill

My back had started to hurt so much that I wondered if I could stand it. The pain and tingling would snake down my legs like electrical charges, and my muscles would go into spasms. I constantly wanted to crack my neck. Things in the plumbing department weren't so good either. What was going on?

Here I was, half way through my freshmen year back at Liggett, learning how to learn in a traditional classroom, and things were going pretty well. Now, we were being told to make appointments down at Cincinnati Children's Hospital to get some answers to my pain and bowel and bladder problems.

The first day of consultations began with the lab, where they stuck you and drew vials of blood. Then a scoliosis X-ray and an abdominal X-ray. Rest assured it's no fun having to drink 16 ounces of fluid before a kidney ultrasound and then having a urodynamics test that measures how efficiently (or inefficiently) your bladder gets emptied. Patients have no privacy! Right?

Next, we had an appointment with Dr. Pramod P. Reddy, a wonderful urologist who had been seeing me since I was 10 years old.[1] He confirmed that my bladder was more than twice the size of a normal 15-year-old's. That didn't account for my present troubles, though. He felt something new was going on, so he ordered more tests.

My family had always appreciated Dr. Reddy's manner and approach. He treated me not as a body part he had to fix, but as a whole person he wanted to show concern for. In fact, he interacted with my whole family that way. He described his philosophy of medicine as *cura personalis*, Latin for care of the whole person.[2]

After Dr. Reddy, we ran up to the eighth floor for an appointment with Dr. Kerry Crone, the pediatric neurosurgeon who had done my tethered cord surgery five years earlier. We described my symptoms. He had seen my latest MRI, done annually at St. John Hospital in Detroit. The reading there was an "all clear" (as in no sign of problems).

Dr. Crone didn't like it, though. Something looked suspicious. When you take an MRI of your spinal column, you're looking to make sure the spinal cord is "floating" in the fluid in the column. The St. John Hospital MRI had been done with me lying on my back, which allowed the cord to kind of lie down in the column—making it harder to verify that it wasn't attached anywhere.

He ordered another MRI, this time with me on my stomach. So, off to radiology we went.

● ● ●

I have always been what nurses call a "hard start" when it comes to getting intravenous therapy (IV) set up in me. "Intravenous" means "into the vein," and I seem to have veins that don't like to volunteer for the process.

In other words, nurses have to poke and prod to find a good vein for an IV and it can be very uncomfortable. Okay, painful.

That's what was happening as they prepped me for the MRI. I needed to have a contrast fluid injected into my system to enhance the appearance of crucial details in the scan. The nurse was having a tough time getting the IV set up.

I admit, my eyes were filling with tears.

"I'm sorry, JT. This must make you afraid," she said, trying to be kind.

I sighed.

"No, Jesus tells us not to be afraid," I said looking up. "This just plain hurts!"

● ● ●

Early the next morning, we hurried back to the pediatric neurosurgery department. Dr. Crone was unavailable, so we met with Mimi, Dr. Crone's nurse and right arm.

Mimi showed us the scan. We could see what the problem was. Right there, on the screen. I started to choke up. *No. Not again.* Mom's eyes watered. Dad swallowed hard.

We left the office and wandered silently to the end of the hall. Tall windows were perpendicular to a wall of elevators, and I remember staring out on Cincinnati through tears. I walked ahead of my folks. My throat was tight and my head was starting to explode. I couldn't hold it in any longer. I broke down crying.

Another tethered cord surgery!

This time I was five years older and knew exactly what I was facing. The most painful surgery I had ever endured. Unlike an operation like intestinal surgery, where the pain and discomfort was localized, the TC procedure produced the agony from head to toe. I was just overwhelmed.

I leaned against the cold window sill and sobbed. I could hear Mom crying too, and Dad was teary.

● ● ●

"JT never dreaded operations. His attitude was always like 'Let's go get it done.' Kinda like a team going out on the field to win," recalls Mom. "This time it was so very different. We all knew what we were up against."

But, we also knew we had no choice. As before, if the situation was not treated, I could be permanently disabled. Even paralyzed.

It hit all of us hard. After all, only 5 percent of tethered-cord patients have it happen again!

● ● ●

Dad took me into the men's room and I splashed my face and blew my nose.

"We're going to take it one day at a time, J," he said. "We'll get through this."

We shuffled down to my next appointment, which happened to be with our dear Dr. Peña. I hadn't seen him since he had redone the Malone procedure on my belly. When he came in to the examination room, something about his kind manner and his knowing my history made it hard to not weep.

It felt like my brain had flown off to Planet Worry. I couldn't concentrate. But still, I had something I wanted to tell him. "Dr. Peña," I said, through sniffles, "I wanted to thank you again for the Malone procedure. It changed my life."

Dr. Peña smiled and gave me a hug. He and his team made us feel so much better. We had to focus on the positive.

• • •

A month later, I walked back into Cincinnati Children's Hospital, hoping for the best. It was 5:30 am, Tuesday, May 17, 2011.

By noon, Dr. Crone came out of the operating room and updated my parents. The lumbar laminectomy, as it is called, went well. There was just a bit of the unexpected.

"Dr. Crone was surprised at what he discovered," remembers Mom. "JT had two spots of tethering at the original spot and slightly below it. He hadn't seen that before."

I, of course, was out of it. My parents came to post-op recovery around 1:30 p.m. and followed me up to my hospital room when I was moved. I was on Dilaudid for the surgical pain and Valium for the back spasms. I was extremely nauseous and throwing up left and right, which only made the spasms worse. The Zofran, given for the nausea, wasn't working.

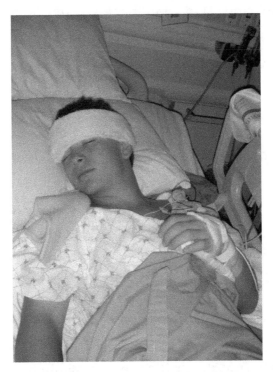

Later that night they tried something for the nausea called Phenergan. Still, I was so horribly uncomfortable that I begged Mom to get a nurse. My head was splitting in two. They increased the Valium and I finally started to rest.

Later, I would read the nurse's report from that evening, which stated "the pain is tight, is constant with flare-ups, is better with medications and worse with movement." Yep.

Dad spent the morning with me, and Mom came in the afternoon. Slowly the Valium helped lessen the spasms, and the Dilaudid reduced the pain.

After Mom and Dad got back from dinner, we had surprise visitors! Papi and Nani, and our family friend, Grace Fenton. They made me smile.

They didn't stay long, though, and I dozed off. Dad spent the night.

The next morning, May 19, Dad already had gotten me out of bed. That meant slowly rolling me on my side, helping me nudge toward the edge of the mattress, guiding my legs toward the floor, pulling my arms gently to help me raise up, and supporting me when I slid to a standing position while bellowing in pain.

By the time Mom came at 10:45 a.m., Dad was helping me "walk" down the hall (it was more like inching, creeping, shuffling!). Dr. Crone and Mimi checked on me, and they were happy with my progress. I now could eat something solid and resume my treatments, but the catheter had to stay in until Dr. Reddy ordered it out.

So, about those treatments.

Yes, I hadn't eaten much, but the last thing I needed was constipation. The thing is, I couldn't bend, so that meant I couldn't use a toilet. Couldn't manage a bedpan either!

You may not want to imagine this scene. It's not pleasant. But, it illustrates what a patient like me has to face. My only option was to do the Malone in the shower.

Poor Dad. Even though I was hanging on to the shower rails with both hands, I couldn't stand alone. I was too shaky. My stomach and intestines were cramping. I was nauseous and ached all over. Dad got into the shower with me and held me steady.

We hung my bag of solution on the shower head and plugged it in to the Malone valve in my belly button. And then we had to stand, waiting, quivering with the cold and pain and discomfort. For half an hour, maybe 45 minutes.

Remember, I have no peristalsis muscles in my bowels so the only way for me to have a bowel movement is to use gravity and my abdominal muscles to push. But those muscles are connected to the back—so every time I pushed in the shower I cried out in pain. My surgical area felt like someone was cutting it with a knife again. Without anesthesia.

The treatment worked, though. Poor Dad cleaned me up, cleaned up the shower and drain, and cleaned himself up. Then we crept back to my bed.

I went back to sleep. I woke up with sharp pain and spasms, got some meds and went back to sleep. Hotpads under me felt good.

Dr. Reddy came by at 7 p.m. and said they needed to measure my urine output until 6 a.m. So, the catheter stayed put.

In the middle of the night I awoke again in pain and with a full bladder. Mom and Dad helped me stand. I peed out 1200 ml. Remember, the normal maximum is 500 ml. Wow.

May 20 was a tough day. I felt horrible. It was good to get the catheter out, but then I felt like I couldn't pee. I was wobbly, sick to my stomach, and loopy. I asked to stop the Valium and Oxycotin (which made me feel as if I was almost hallucinating!) and went with Tylenol and Zofran.

The next day I felt better and was eating. The best news was that I was going to be able to go home tomorrow!

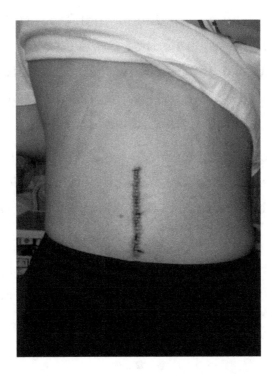

• • •

When we climbed into my Papi's plane to go home, I got a wonderful surprise. There sat two of my very best friends from Detroit! Andrew and Kyle!

The ordeal had been as bad as I dreaded it would be. But, now it felt so good to be just a kid rather than a patient. I had to stretch out between the seats, but we laughed all the way home.

When we landed at the municipal airport in Detroit, Andrew's wonderful mom—I called her Aunt Sue—and his whole family were by their car parked alongside the runway. They had a megaphone screaming "Welcome Home!"

When we got home we found that Liggett had sent a bundle of bright balloons that towered over my head. A big poster board that said WELCOME HOME JT! came with it. It was covered with get-well wishes from classmates, teachers, and administrators.

I hadn't thought about school for a long time! Before the surgery, my parents had said Liggett decided to let my final grade be whatever I had earned by the time of the operation.

I would have to make up a few things during the summer, but hey! I had made it through my first year of high school!

• • •

On Friday, June 3, 2011, my folks and I returned to Liggett for Class Day. It was great to see friends and walk around campus. The big event was an end-of-year awards assembly in the auditorium.

I sat uncomfortably, clapping as classmates heard their names called and went up to the stage for their awards. Knowing my academic situation, I had no expectations and was just fine with that.

The next award was the TiJuan Kidd Prize. TiJuan Kidd ('90) was a sophomore who tragically died in the summer of 1987. The prize is given annually to a ninth grader "who, with positive contagious energy, exemplifies the qualities TiJuan possessed: honesty, determination, confidence, and dependability."

Then I heard Dr. Healey call out my name.

I froze and looked at Mom and Dad. They had surprised looks on their faces and then they broke into smiles. When I went up to the stage, all I remember was hearing the room full of my peers clapping.

All the fears, anxiety, worry, and pain I had experienced this year just melted away.

Chapter 28

GRIT

The mountain is never as big as it appears. You're never as small as you believe.

— Steve Maraboli

Ladi's headlights bounced off the evergreens lining the dirt road we'd taken south of Minturn. I glanced in the back seat of the khaki-colored Jeep Wrangler Rubicon. Yep, Ladi's son, Dominik, was asleep. I would have been, too, but I was too excited.

After healing from my second tethered cord surgery, I had set a goal to climb my second fourteener as soon as I could, and now it was happening!

A fourteener is a mountain whose elevation is 14,000 feet or more. The United States has 96 fourteeners, all west of the Mississippi River. The state with the most is, you guessed it, Colorado! It has 58 of the 96,[1] and it is on my bucket list to climb all 58.

Ladi had come up with the idea the afternoon before. My parents and I were having a late lunch with him and his family at Moe's Original BBQ in Eagle. We had all just gotten back from kayaking on the Shoshone Rapids on the Colorado River near Glenwood Springs.

"JT, why don't we go climb Holy Cross?" Ladi said. He knew of my goal, and the famous Mount of the Holy Cross[2] was the nearest one.

"Sure!" I said, looking at Mom and Dad. "When?"

"Tomorrow. We'll leave at 2 a.m."

I laughed. I'd known Ladi too long to be surprised. He's always ready for an adventure.

"That way we'll get to the summit while the weather is still safe," said Ladi, grinning, "and we can avoid dying."

● ● ●

Ladi—who was then a member of the Vail search-and-rescue team[3] and knew his stuff—wasn't exaggerating. Much.

My family had spent enough time in Colorado to understand that you have to take its weather seriously. It was August, and summer in the high country has a reputation for rapid, dangerous changes. Sunshine on a summit can transform in minutes into a freezing rain. The biggest danger are the thunder storms. You simply do not want to be caught at high elevation when there's any possibility of lightning.[4]

Dangerous too was the rugged land. Holy Cross Wilderness was known for its steep trails, uneven terrain, loose talus, and hidden cliffs. Ladi knew of a woman in 2005 who got separated from her hiking partner and was never seen again, despite the largest search ever organized in the state at the time. Five years later another person disappeared.[5]

I'd faced scary situations before. But, in the wilderness things can happen that you have no control over. I love being in nature. But how would I handle today's challenge?

We raced home to get our supplies,[6] pack our daypacks, and hit the hay. After a short night, Ladi and Dominik, who was 10, picked me up. I was glad Dominik was coming on the hike too. This would be his second fourteener too: his first was when he was two and a half years old!

We headed in the moonlight to Tigiwon Road, an eight-mile-long Forest Service road off Highway 24. Tigiwon is a Ute Indian word for "friends." Five bumpy miles up the rut-filled road, at around 10,000 feet elevation, the headlights glanced off an old structure. It looked like a log cabin on a big stone foundation.

"Ladi, what is that?" I asked.

"It's the Tigiwon Community House.[7] It was built back in the 1930s as a shelter for pilgrims coming here to see the Mount of the Holy Cross and worship God," he said.

I felt a little like a pilgrim this morning. Thanking God for my renewed health. Seeking a deeper relationship with Him.

A few more miles and Tigiwon Road dead-ended at Half Moon Campground. Here, was also the trailheads of two trails, starting at 10,320 feet. We parked, and Ladi woke up Dominik.

The shortest and most commonly traveled way to reach the summit of Holy Cross is known as the Standard Route, or North Ridge. You start from the trailhead and take Half Moon Pass Trail. After a steep climb of a few miles, you reach Half Moon Pass at 11,600 feet. Then you descend into the East Cross Creek Basin, where some hikers spend a night before continuing up the North Ridge and to the peak. Most people then backtrack to the trailhead the way they came.

Another, longer, way takes you from the Half Moon Campground via the Fall Creek Trail up a few miles to Notch Mountain Trail at 11,100 feet, ending up on top of Notch Mountain Ridge at 13,000 feet. Now, you're on the opposite rim of a huge bowl from Holy Cross, giving you a stunning view of the peak across a gigantic expanse. Some hikers make this their destination. Others continue to hike two more miles over a giant backbone known as

Halo Ridge. That requires you to get past three thirteeners and a talus-filled saddle along the ridge before you can ascend Holy Cross. Not many hikers take this route.

You can then turn around and descend the Fall Creek-Notch Mountain track down to your vehicle. Or you can catch the Standard Route, making a full—and long—loop known as the Halo Ridge Trail.

It all sounds pretty simple on paper, doesn't it? But it's a bit more challenging, boots on the ground. I was glad we were going to just do the Standard Route.

● ● ●

The trick to long hikes, I've learned, is to outsmart your own mind. Maybe that's a trick to a lot of things in life, too.

After Ladi registered us at the trailhead, we layered our outerwear against the close-to-freezing temperatures. Then we put on our headlamps, loaded up our water and daypacks, and started off. It was 4 a.m. Pitch dark. Ladi had climbed Holy Cross a number of times, but Dominik and I had no idea what we were facing. Good thing.

The first leg of the climb was pretty steep. I wanted to stop and look at the amazing stars, but I had to keep my headlamp pointed down on the rocky trail. Besides,

Dominik was keeping up with Ladi, so I was determined not to fall behind.

In an hour or so it felt as if we were reaching the top of something.

"Ladi, is that the summit?" I asked.

He chuckled. "You'll see a lot of false summits in life," he said. "You're not even close."

Oh.

We had only reached Half Moon Pass, which is 11,060 feet. I was awake now, and the horizon was starting to glow with some pink.

After dawn broke open, I loved seeing the dew glistening on the grass and bushes. Birds started to chirp. We came across big patches of snow, so of course we had to have a snowball fight. But not for long. Ladi said we needed to push on.

Descending the couple of thousand feet into the East Cross Creek drainage took a few hours. The temperatures rose. I spotted douglas fir, bristlecone pine, engelmann spruce, and other conifers. The undergrowth was thick with alder, mountain ash, willow, and dwarf juniper. A waterfall cut through the middle of the basin. On the creek basin's north flank were steep granite walls. Holy Cross was to the south of us.

After a long climb up from the creek we reached a tree line and a rocky field, which required a lot of scrambling and bouldering. I was getting tired. I know Dominik was too.

Too bad. Here's where we had to practice that mind-over-mind trick. "Ignore your fatigue," said Ladi. "One foot in front of another."

I smiled at Dominik. Both of us had heard his dad say that many times.

We kept our eyes peeled for the little rock statues that mark the trail. The terrain narrowed to a prominent notch at 13,700 feet. Then on and up. *Almost there. Almost there.*

Then at 10 a.m., we finally reached the summit of the Mount of the Holy Cross. From this approach hikers can't see the giant cracks that formed the snow-filled cross. But it didn't matter. You could scan a cloudless horizon 36 degrees for miles and miles. It was like you were on top of the world. It was amazing!

After taking some photographs we propped up against some granite boulders, gulped water, and ate a snack. Boy, did it taste good.

Then Ladi raised a question.

"All right, boys. Should we return the way we came? Or should we tackle the Halo Route?"

● ● ●

Try as I might, I couldn't think of any reason not to do Halo. The sky was clear, and it was only 10:30 a.m. We'd have to cover nine miles instead of six, but four of them would be in the forest—meaning lightning would be less of a danger.

Dominik, his straight blond hair falling over his eyes, didn't say anything.

"All right! Let's do it!" said Ladi, jumping up.

On the other side of the summit we saw the start of the saddle that was Halo Ridge. The elevation dropped steeply on both sides of us. Shining below on our left, on the south end of the Cross Creek drainage, was the Bowl of Tears lake. It truly was a beautiful view.

"Dad. There's a man," said Dominik.

A solitary hiker was ahead of us maybe a quarter of a mile.

"Helloooo!" bellowed Ladi, raising his arm. The man turned.

"Where are you headed?" Ladi yelled.

The man called back: *Halo Route.* Ladi asked if he knew the way. He said yes, waved, turned, and continued on.

"I guess he's not interested in joining us," said Ladi, shaking his head.

We kept moving. Some of the stones we had to climb over now were as big as VW cars! Dominik occasionally needed a boost, then we'd jump down from the tops.

I noticed that Ladi kept his eye on the man ahead. All of a sudden, he gave a quick yell.

"Wrong direction!"

The guy had taken a spur off the main trail. One reason the Halo Route is more challenging than North Ridge is because the trail is virtually unmarked at the top. It's easy to get disoriented in the moonscape-like talus.

"He's going to get lost. Or worse," said Ladi. "Stay here. Hunker down and look after each other."

He ran off and we lost sight of him. Dominik and I looked at each other. "Let's find a safe spot to wait in," I said.

I don't know how long Ladi was gone—maybe 20 minutes, maybe half an hour—before he jogged back into view. Dominik jumped up and they gave each other a little sideways hug.

"He's back on track," said Ladi, smiling.

I could see, though, that Ladi still looked concerned. The detour with the hiker had taken up more time than he had wanted, and clouds were building in the sky.

Glancing up, he was blunt. "We need to pick up the pace and get the hell out of here."

• • •

Later Ladi would tell us that he knew we were on the verge of exhaustion, and he was thinking of options, should things go bad. "Whenever you're faced with danger, it's not the end of the world," he would say. "There are opportunities to overcome danger and learn from it."

Dominik and I could tell that Ladi was serious, and we silently agreed to speed ourselves up.

In about an hour or so, after countless zigzags on rock-filled slopes under darkening skies, we reached the back side of Notch Mountain, where Ladi knew there was an emergency shelter, equipped with a lightning rod.

What a relief. I was so tired I was oblivious to the cool structure of the historic Notch Mountain Shelter,[8] a hut made of stones (of course!). Inside was a large room, a giant fireplace, and narrow split-log benches. No provisions—but protection. We were safe if a storm started.

We collapsed on the rough benches or the dusty concrete floor. Every muscle ached. Everyone was silent.

Then another concern: I discovered I was low on water. I didn't say anything.

The large windows on the front of the hut framed the Mount of the Holy Cross. I just stared at it for a while.

"The clouds have cleared," said Ladi. "We can go."

Dominik and I looked at him for a moment. Then it dawned on us we had to get up and get moving.

"C'mon, JT," Dominik sighed. "Just five more miles."

● ● ●

We were at tree level now. Ladi started cutting through the three dozen switchbacks to save time.

I drank the last drop of water from my Camelback.

Ladi kept saying, *We're almost there. Keep moving. We're almost there. Keep moving.*

The trail leveled out. Trees formed a canopy over us. Then, we spotted the trailhead, the parking area. It was 2:51 p.m. We had been on this adventure for roughly 12 hours.

It started to rain.

Dominik and I were never more happy to sit in that old Jeep. We guzzled water from an emergency supply Ladi kept in the vehicle.

He was smiling. "What you've done today you should feel proud about," Ladi said. "Most adults couldn't do what you did."[9]

Dominik and I didn't have the energy to do more than nod.

"We live a pretty risk-free life," Ladi later said. "Not many dangers, yes? But in nature, we are exposed to danger. It's good training. You learn you have to have grit to handle anything."

I know now that it's also crucial to have the right people around you—to push you, give you courage, and watch your back. That's what Dominik and I did for each other that day. Ladi too.

When we got home, this tired pilgrim showered, had dinner, then went to bed and slept for 11 hours.

Chapter 29

THE COME-BACK KID

But all endings are also beginnings. We just don't know it at the time.

— Mitch Albom

"Careful, Mrs. Minwalla! Grab the rail on the stern. My dad will help you."

A teacher from my school was going on a boat ride with my father and me. But, it wasn't a typical trip, and this wasn't a typical boat, and she wasn't a typical teacher.

At Liggett, all Upper School students must choose a topic they're interested in and spend two years researching it as part of the school's mandatory Academic Research Program (ARP). Seniors then make a formal presentation of their findings.

You might think that assignment would be a challenge to someone like me. It was!

But, I had come a long way from that nervous ninth grader who had no idea how—or if—he was going to make it in high school.

And, Liggett had changed too.

"JT was as much of an opportunity for Liggett, as Liggett was for JT," recalls Jay Trevorrow, who served as director of technology while I was there. "He helped us all learn to become more effective educators."

That sounds pretty lofty, doesn't it? I think Mr. Trevorrow was referring to a bunch of factors coming together at just the right time, almost like divine timing. And I was lucky enough to play a small part as a catalyst.

● ● ●

The first and most important factor was the new Head of School, Dr. Healey, who first appeared in my story in chapter 25. He saw a need for Liggett to become more open to children who learned in unconventional ways.

My English teacher, Mr. Andy Knote, put it this way.

"The intellectual and academic diversity of the student body has increased a lot since JT came in," said Mr. Knote. "Dr. Healey changed the identity of the school in a number of ways and [that] was one of the main ones."

Mr. Knote, who has taught at Liggett for two decades, acknowledged the change was not easy. "But with JT in particular, . . . he was such a hard worker and he was so responsible, that it really made the process easier."

Another factor was Mr. Trevorrow, who had worked with Dr. Healey and Mrs. Beckmann for many years in New York City. He brought with him a willingness to recognize that it was acceptable, and sometimes crucial, to learn using a whole set of nontraditional tools.

"JT is really good visually. He does great video. So, I thought, let's look at the guy's strengths, and then make information available to him in ways that speak to his strengths," explained Mr. Trevorrow, who had been a classroom teacher of English and Latin for 20 years before becoming an assistive technology[1] expert.

I'm very grateful to all the Liggett educators who were willing to try new things for my sake, and for the sake of kids that came after me. Those four years in high school were trial and error, on all sides!

There were big changes, like audio books and dictation software. There were small ones, like using email instead of handwritten communication, or letting me use my cell phone to take a photo of homework assignments listed on the classroom smart board instead of being required to hand-copy them. (It takes me forever to write.)

Along the way, I got better at advocating for myself, and, I'm told, the faculty also shifted in their perceptions and practices.

"This was a two-way street working with JT," said Mr. Trevorrow. "We, the so-called professionals, had to be as open to learning and trying as he was."

● ● ●

Not everyone was as positive.

On my first visit to Mrs. Beckmann's office I noticed a photograph of her with a student towering over her. They both were smiling big. "Who's that?" I asked.

She told me about Forrest. "At my school in New York, we took in a seventh grader who also had learning issues. I kind of shepherded him through. He ended up at Princeton," she said.

That made an impression! I told my parents about that photo and said, "I want to be the Forrest of Liggett."

It was my junior year, 2013, and we were giving some thought to me actually attending college. It was time to meet with the director of college guidance and ask for recommendations for schools she thought I should apply to.

Independently, I had decided I wanted to apply to all sorts of colleges—even Ivy League schools like Princeton. Yes, it was a long shot, but why not try?

At my appointment with the counselor, not only did her list not include Ivy League schools, it didn't have any institutions that would be a challenge for me. I asked her about that.

I'm certain she didn't mean to be as unkind as it sounded. But her blunt reply showed her low expectations of me: "Why waste your time, JT?"

● ● ●

I wasn't going to accept low expectations.

Julie Martin Kelly, the daughter of my homeschool teacher, Mrs. Martin, became my tutor in ninth grade. Julie, who was training to be a teacher, would come to my house four nights a week to work with me on assignments and help me stay organized. (Now married and a mom, she tutored me until I graduated from college—a total of eight years!)

I continued to meet with Steve Tattum whenever he was in town, maybe four times a year. I would join him when he trained Michigan educators on his reading program, sharing my story and demonstrating my current level of progress.

Steve also volunteered to talk with Beth Beckmann and Dr. Ondersma at Liggett to give them background on my dyslexia and learning differences, and on his recommended interventions.

"But, I had become somewhat irrelevant by then," he recalls, "because JT had become his own advocate. He had become confident about asking for help and accommodations when it came to what he could and couldn't do."

● ● ●

Every senior class plans some sort of gift to the school. A friend, Ellene, and I came up with the idea of renovating the senior commons area in the Upper School. It was a popular gathering place for seniors, but it was kind of worn. So, we spent a year raising $10,000.

Meanwhile, I had to pull together all my advocating and accommodating and tutoring and hard work to tackle Liggett's Academic Research Program. It was a little overwhelming.

The upside, though, was that Mrs. Minwalla had approved my topic: marine propulsion. Not a big surprise for a choice, right? After all, I had grown up on boats and loved everything about them.

But, researching and organizing the research was way beyond my comfort zone. Julie helped as I narrowed the topic down to pod drives, a new way of powering pleasure boats. I interviewed manufacturers like Volvo and Caterpillar, and compared the pros and cons with the traditional shaft-line systems. One of the major advantages was a joystick that helped captains maneuver their craft in tight spots.

Around this time the Grosse Pointe Yacht Club was participating in a boat show. I got the idea of asking to "borrow" a 42-foot Palm Beach boat from the dealer for my presentation. Amazingly, they said yes!

The day after I presented my findings at school, Dad and I met Mrs. Minwalla at the yacht club. It was early May and sunny, but breezy. Being on the water was outside *her* comfort zone, so I appreciated her coming.

Two Palm Beach representatives were aboard, as well. One would be at the helm as I explained all about the pod systems.

The floating docks were crowded with boats in their slips, because of the boat show. That gave us a great chance to show off how easy it is to maneuver a boat with pod drives. Then we headed out to open waters on Lake St. Clair, and I talked and talked. At the end of my report, the reps were a little surprised at how much I knew about boating. One teased and said, "Want a job?"

Actually, they did offer me an internship—in Australia! I had to turn it down, but it was encouraging to get professional affirmation after all the hard work.

Mrs. Minwalla, who is now Liggett's Assistant Head of Upper School and Dean of Student Life, said she enjoyed the report. And the cruise.

• • •

A month later, on Sunday, June 8, 2014, I graduated from the school that years before had kicked me out. *Cum laude.*[2]

I was beyond excited, and relieved! When I got my diploma on stage Dr. Healey gave me a big smile and a bear hug.

All the years of picking myself up after getting knocked down; all the times of feeling odd and different from my friends; all the thousands of hours of trying and failing and trying again; all the pushing through suffering and pain and physical limitations to be strong and free; all the prayers—all of it turned out to be worth it.

That was my biggest lesson: Don't let anyone tell you that you can't accomplish something. Don't ever give up. Don't ever give up. Don't ever give up!

Chapter 30

EXTRAORDINARY

*To be a great person, walk hand in hand and side
by side with great people.*

— Dr. Nido R. Qubein,
President, High Point University

Gold letters spelled HIGH POINT UNIVERSITY across the
campus entrance. They shimmered in the late afternoon
sunlight. The clock in the white and brick cupola atop the
guard house said 5:45.

After our flight to the Carolinas, Dad suggested driving
to the three colleges for which we had tours scheduled
the next day, just to see where they were and to check
them out. High Point was the last one we were swinging
by before dinner.

"Mom! Dad! Check that out!"

Just past the entrance we saw a small cluster of four-
foot-high purple signs set amongst some nice

landscaping. They were labeled RESERVED PARKING FOR SPECIAL GUEST. I glanced at their LED screens.

Guess they were expecting us!

JT Mestdagh
University Liggett
Grosse Pointe, MI

Dad parked the rental car and we started strolling. We saw a beautiful meticulously manicured campus, no doubt about it. Massive neo-classical brick buildings were connected by curving paths alongside dark green lawns. Leafy trees arched over benches and fountains as late afternoon was turning into early evening. Faint classical music was coming from somewhere.

There was something about the atmosphere that already was drawing me. I could see myself here.

"Why don't we go look at the Phillips School of Business, J? Get a feel for it," said Dad. "The map says it's right over there."

We spotted a stately two-story structure. Four giant white columns at its entrance held up a wide portico topped by a triangular pediment. We stepped inside. Everything looked new and elegant.

We returned to the promenade, a wide central greenway lined with international flags.

I already was certain.

"I'm going here," I said quietly.

• • •

We actually knew very little about High Point University, a 90-year-old liberal arts institution in the Piedmont Triad region of North Carolina. No family friends or children of friends had attended. No college advisor had had experience with it. But the school's website described a program for students with learning differences (something on our inventory of "must haves"). So, since we were going to be in the vicinity, we added High Point to the bottom of our list of colleges worth visiting.

I was doing well at University Liggett School. But by now you know that essays and test scores—typical college admission requirements—weren't my strong suit. Would any college even consider me?

And even if I got into a college, would it be a mountain too high to climb?

Later Mom would admit that her heart dropped when I made my little announcement. After all, 10,000 kids would be applying for 1,400 spaces. Could there really be a spot for a guy with severe dyslexia, poor writing skills, and short-term memory loss?

Directly across from the business building was a smaller structure, this one topped with a white steeple. Just then its large white front doors swung open and people began to stream out.

"J, let's go over there and see how the kids interact with each other," Dad said.

It was the end of chapel, held every Wednesday at 5:30 p.m. (The school has roots in the Methodist tradition.) As we watched, a distinguished-looking man walked among the students, smiling and chatting. Then he spotted us.

"Hey, I think that's the president of the university," whispered Dad.

● ● ●

President Nido R. Qubein was born in the Middle East. Fatherless at six, he came to the United States as a teenager with $50 in his pocket. He learned English. After earning a college degree (at High Point College— before it became a university) and doing graduate studies, he built a career as a businessman, entrepreneur, consultant, and motivational speaker.[1] Then in 2005, he was invited to become the university president.

It was obvious that Dr. Qubein was enthusiastic about High Point. He described its growth, its future plans, and its focus on promoting the values of "God, Family, Country."

He spelled out how the school emphasized excellence and high goals and big dreams. I liked that. I could tell Mom and Dad did too.

Dr. Qubein talked for 45 minutes with us, a family he knew nothing about. I would later hear him tell students to never miss a chance to stop and talk with someone. He was all about relationships.

Eventually he suggested we try one of the campus restaurants, and offered to drive us to it. Then his cell phone rang.

It was his wife, asking him where he was. The whole family was waiting for him to come home so they could celebrate the birthday of one of his sons!

Dr. Qubein laughed and said he'd better get going. But first, he gave us that ride.

● ● ●

When we reached the fourth floor of R. G. Wanek Center and found the restaurant, we were a little blown away.

Not only because Dr. Qubein had made a reservation for us and said the meal was paid for, but because we were standing in a quiet walnut-paneled, white-tableclothed, candle-lit American steakhouse.

In a university?

A man in a dark suit greeted us and introduced himself as Tim. He was the general manager of the restaurant, called 1924 PRIME. He seated us and handed us menus.

On one side of the menu were items you'd find in any traditional chop house. On the other were appetizers and entrees from China. Mom asked Tim about that.

He smiled. He explained that HPU never missed a chance to teach. What looked like just a high-end restaurant was also an immersive learning lab.

"Having meals in 1924 PRIME enabled students to gain etiquette skills they needed to excel in their careers," he said. For example, students made reservations as part of their meal plan a week in advance "as if they were making plans for a business meal." They had to follow a dress code, and cell phones were not allowed. They had to practice (or learn!) good table manners, like, which utensils to use when, and how to pass a bread basket!

As to the non-American food, PRIME highlighted a different country every month and featured its cuisine. Printed on the menus was information about the chosen country and its culture, and tips on customs centered around sharing a meal. The idea was that HPU graduates were likely to go on to careers all over the world. Understanding how to handle oneself in another culture was crucial.

Did you know that at business banquets in China, it's considered impolite not to sample everything that's offered? We had a great meal that night!

● ● ●

"Hey Dad, Mom. There's a big envelope in the mail from High Point!"

The odds of my being accepted into High Point University had seemed too high to even hope. But deep down I felt I was supposed to go there. It was just a feeling, like a tap on the shoulder from the Holy Spirit. It turned out to be right.

"We were all surprised JT was accepted," my mother says. "It was another God thing. It had to be."

Part of the appeal for me was that HPU did not use the term "special education." The program that oversaw academic support and accommodations was called Learning Excellence.[2]

HPU fosters a positive orientation in every detail of its campus, down to calling the hard-working maintenance and custodial crew the "campus enhancement team." Maybe that seems like just playing with words—like calling a used car a "previously enjoyed" vehicle. But, for someone who had been slapped with labels all his life, it was a breath of fresh air.

My parents understood the significance, and they sensed the same awareness in the school administration. A talk by President Qubein during a Parents' Weekend left a big impression on them.

A huge screen behind him was covered with a long list of human characteristics that are valuable, but aren't measurable by traditional testing. Traits like creativity, reliability, empathy, self-awareness, courage. . . His list was long.

It brought tears to Mom's eyes. "Here was an environment, a culture we had hoped JT would find," she remembers, "an extension of the values of our home."

She also thought of Proverbs 22:6. "Train up a child in the way he should go, even when he is old he will not depart from it" (NAS). I wasn't old yet, but I was well "trained" and had accepted these values as my own, too—or else I wouldn't have wanted to come to HPU.

High Point's emphasis on valuing all people and finding ways to help them grow and excel reminded my parents of the stance Dr. Healey had taken at Liggett. For too long schools have relied on "standardized" testing and quantifiable systems and predictable formulas—which leaves unique students out. That's really too bad, because people with learning differences often become our most successful entrepreneurs.

Being accepted into HPU gave me a chance to climb a crucial hurdle and see new paths for my life, and for that I'm very, very grateful.

It was a four-year-long uphill battle, though. I won't deny that.

● ● ●

Freshman Orientation Weekend was a little overwhelming. Lots of information to take in, people to meet and remember, places to find. Every new student in the history of higher education probably feels disoriented like I did, but I had to work extra hard at keeping organized.

Mom and Dad were at the weekend, too. At a few events I happened to notice a guy sitting, not with someone that looked like a mother or father, but with another guy. They looked alike so I took them to be brothers or cousins.

Later, while waiting for our flight at Piedmont Triad International Airport in Greensboro (we were making a quick trip to Papi and Nani's in south Florida), Dad spotted those same two guys sitting a little way from us. They were waiting to board the same plane!

"J, introduce yourself," Dad suggested. "Maybe he could be your roommate."

I leaned forward and said hi. The guy's name was Tristan. He was traveling with his older brother, Austin. "My parents wanted to come but they had a commitment," Tristan said, smiling. "Plus Mom thought I would prefer not having them 'tag along'."

That's how Tristan and I became roommates for four years. The first year we lived in the dorm called University Center II. We spent year two, three, and four at Centennial Square II, which was a townhouse where we lived with five other guys, all who stuck together and became good friends.

● ● ●

Every freshman is enrolled in a fall semester course, called Life Skills. Taught by Dr. Qubein himself, it's very practical. The topics include how to build self-esteem, learn time management and set goals, understand the basics of leadership, handle personal finances, communicate effectively, and live healthy.

Every student was assigned to a "freshman success coach": a trained staff member who becomes an academic advisor, life coach, sounding board, cheerleader, and friend. I wish every young person could be blessed this way!

In August 2014 I met mine: a wonderful man named Dr. Akir Khan. In the first meeting with my parents and me, he instantly understood my situation.

"I want you to know I'll always have your back, JT," said Dr. Khan, a sharply dressed, confident man who had worked for the George W. Bush administration as a liaison to the Muslim community before coming to High Point. "I've experienced similar things. For example, I had bad enough asthma that I couldn't be in sports or join the military like I wanted to. I never let it stop me but it was hard. That's why I'm thrilled today to be a mentor to students and help them develop their game plans."

Akir (as he told me to address him) and I would meet every week. Together we'd come up with ideas for how to tackle my assignments, my hurdles, my fears. He gave me insight into all the resources HPU offered, and encouraged me to not give up, even when I felt defeated.

"JT has what I call a growth mindset," said Akir. "He has an ability to adapt to his situations, and be willing to be uncomfortable in order to learn outside the box and grow."

I had always tried to be my own advocate when it came to explaining my situation and searching for ways to accomplish what I needed to, despite my limits.

But, college was a new game! The increase in the scale of the challenges—for all students, but especially someone like me—was like hiking a 2,000-foot hill versus climbing Mt. Kilimanjaro (which was on my very long bucket list!)

The student—not the parents, nor anyone else—is the one who must communicate his or her disability needs. The student, not the university, is the one who asks for academic accommodations,[3] gets them approved, informs professors, and then negotiates how it all plays out.

My accommodations letter stated that I could record the lecture in class. I could request copies of lecture notes. I was allowed textbooks "in an alternate format," in other words, versions I could listen to while reading. For course exams, I could take tests in a distraction-reduced place, be able to have software that read the exam to me and recorded my oral responses, and have extended time to take the test.

In every single course I ever took during all those four years at High Point, my accommodations made the difference between failing and passing.

● ● ●

Here's an example. The first semester, I enrolled in a history course, "American Aspirations." History wasn't a strength of mine, but it looked interesting and the professor had a great reputation.

The amount of reading was tough, though, even with audio books. I talked it over with Julie Martin Kelly, my tutor from home. I conferred with my Learning Excellence academic coach, Heather Slocum. And I made sure to reach out to the professor, Dr. Kara Dixon Vuic.

"This particular professor," remembers Mrs. Slocum, "understood that JT had a hard time getting all of his ideas down on paper, but could explain things better verbally. She made arrangements for JT to arrive early to class when they were going to have a quiz or test so that he could utilize his extra-time accommodation. Then she would stay with him after class so that he could review his answers orally with her."

It was so great that Dr. Vuic gave me this encouraging experience during my first semester! She was an example of how HPU professors agreed to work with me. Mrs. Slocum says it's because they saw I was willing to put in hard work. But, not all my early experiences were as encouraging.

One accommodation I had not thought to ask for was use of a calculator for a test. Being able to have that tool was the only way I passed my high school math and science classes. The rule in college, though, was no calculators for exams. Period.

When I approached the professor of my first mathematics course at HPU, she would not budge. She wasn't unkind, but she said rules were rules.

So, of course I failed the first big exam. I knew the concepts, but I just couldn't work fast enough. I felt pretty bad.

Akir, Julie, and my folks all encouraged me not to give up. I made an appointment with Mrs. Slocum. I was able to request a modification of my accommodations letter. This version would include the right to have a calculator with me for tests.

I went back to the professor with the new letter and asked to retake the exam. Nope. She said no. No retest.

Boy, that totally bummed me out. Maybe college was going to challenge me even more than I had expected.

● ● ●

One area that was working out was the social realm. All the guys in my dorm were great. In fact, a bunch of us—like Tristan, Dylan, Beau, Nicholas F., Nick F., Nick M., and Nico (yeah, that got a little confusing sometimes!)—would live together in a college townhouse the rest of our time at HPU. They all helped me out tremendously, in more ways than I can describe—from studying with me to supporting my medical challenges. We became brothers and I'm sure we'll remain close the rest of our lives.

In the spring term of freshman year Tristan, Beau, and I rushed Pi Kappa Phi fraternity. We finally convinced Nico to join us the following year, too. (Getting Nico to come live with us might have involved a few pranks, I mean "persuasion!")

Nico was in Learning Excellence with me. We had the same math tutor. He had to work hard at writing and reading comprehension, too. But we had more in common than learning challenges and we just clicked.

We discovered a shared love of being active. (Ladi and I taught Nico, a snowboarder, how to ski!) In fact, a bunch of guys frequently came on break to my family's place in Beaver Creek, Colorado, to ski.

Concerts, "night life," service projects, going fishing, mountain-biking, just hanging out—I felt surrounded by great friends.

I also was thrilled to be chosen to be one of the university's Ambassadors. The application process was very competitive. The job gave me an opportunity to strengthen my interpersonal communication skills—plus I got paid for it!

● ● ●

One of my biggest take-aways at college was gaining a deeper awareness of what I can and cannot do well, and how to compensate. It was very stressful, but an ultimately valuable lesson.

My teachers would email their lecture notes and I'd have my software program read the notes to me. But, my comprehension isn't awesome. Julie had copies of all my textbooks and assignments, and she helped me break down all the information and zero in on what I needed to know.

With my short-term memory deficit, it's also very hard for me to recall things I've read or been told. So, Julie has helped me develop systems to aid that. I use a lot of color coding. Red means STUDY THIS!

Julie also helped with time management. We met by Skype Monday through Thursday. Working with her gave me confidence.

Especially for oral presentations. We would practice and practice and practice. I'm sure she got tired—I did!—but she never let it show.

"In the last years I felt more like his assistant than his tutor," Julie says, laughing. "He was getting it."

● ● ●

Whenever I got push-back from someone who didn't believe I really needed accommodations or who maybe assumed I was just freeloading or something—I had two choices.

I could get discouraged or even angry. Or, I could go find someone who was positive, who would uplift me or coach me or push me. It was up to me.

In addition to receiving help from Julie, I practically moved into the Learning Excellence offices. Well, not really. But, I did spend a lot of time there. I'm so grateful for people like Mrs. Slocum, Suzanne Hawks, Dr. Craig Curty, and Pamala Wannamaker. They made my college career possible!

Mrs. Slocum created weekly to-do lists; made a semester-at-a-glance calendar to map out tests, papers, projects due, etc.; and put together study plans for the major tests. She also helped me review material, especially vocabulary. And occasionally she read and scribed for me during a midterm or a final.

Those tests were indeed a major, well, test!

"In his freshman year JT was devastated to earn a low grade on a test. He thought it defined him as a student,"

Mrs. Slocum recalled. "Over time he learned that we could talk about the way that he prepared for the test, and then come up with a new plan for the next test."

Mrs. Wannamaker says that when she met me, during my sophomore year, I was still pretty anxious about school. I think she's right. It's ironic, because the fall semester of my junior year was the one time I got on the Dean's List!

Mrs. Wannamaker went to bat for me. "I ordered additional evaluations with a new psychologist," she said, "leading to updated accommodations that limited courses to three instead of four. That helped with JT's confidence."

The next year, as a junior, I was asked to join one of the oldest academic honors at the university called the Order of the Lamp. Students were selected based on scholarship, leadership, character and overall service to the university.

So, yes, my confidence grew. But the work was still demanding and nonstop. Marathoners may know they can run those 26.2 miles, but they still have to push and pant and sweat!

● ● ●

In a one-and-one meeting late in my senior year with the university chaplain, the Rev. Preston Davis, he and I talked about suffering. He acknowledged all that I had gone through growing up, and described how hard times shape us. We get to choose if it's for good or bad.

"In the case of a challenging situation, we might ask, 'Will this make me bitter or will this make me more empathetic to others who are challenged?' From our brief time together I think you've been able to do more of the latter," he said. I appreciated his wise words.

Preston followed with an email in which he wrote, "[A positive attitude] takes pain and turns it into hope. It takes suffering and turns into sight that sees everything as a gift. I pray you tap into that more. Meditate on this gift and I believe you will meditate on none other than God."

● ● ●

All the self-advocacy, time management, study strategies, positive support, and just plain hard work made it possible to pass one of the university's toughest courses: Quantitative Methods.

My dread started the first day. Word problems after word problems. Formulas, tables, Greek letters to represent quantities (I had enough trouble with English letters!). I studied hard.

Then the results of the first test were passed out. After class I went up to the professor, Brielle Tyree. "May I talk with you?"

As I spoke I suddenly got tears in my eyes, because this class was so important and so tough, and I had little hope that I would be able to pass it.

Professor Tyree knew nothing about me. She only knew I had gotten a "very low F—not even close to a D minus," as she put it. I introduced myself, my situation, and my accommodations. She was willing to take a second look at my work. We figured out the biggest problem was the reading of the test itself.

She laid out a plan. I was to come to her office during office hours every day I could, every week until the end of the semester; get tutoring through Learning Excellence; and start study sessions with friends also in the course.

Then she said something that gave me hope.

"If you put the effort into it, you're going to pass this course."

Every week we went one-on-one for three hours, probably more. "I had him talk me through some of the text [in the problems]," said Professor Tyree, "and had him explain his thinking on each problem. He knew the concepts."

By the end of midterm, I had raised my course grade to . . . D minus.

When it came to tests, Professor Tyree said I could have as long as I needed. For the midterm exam, I worked on it for *five hours*. I got really tired! And it wasn't as long as the final was going to be.

After many more weeks of study, I had to face down my fears and take the final exam for Quantitative Methods. Mrs. Hawks let me into the small soundproof room next to her office, where I took most of the college exams. It has specialized software that reads the test out loud and lets me dictate answers into the computer.

Professor Tyree, who lived an hour and a half from High Point's campus, couldn't be around to answer questions. So, she gave me a cell phone number to call if I needed too. (I did!)

"He'd be stuck on what a certain phrase meant," Professor Tyree recalls. "I'd ask him, 'What are you thinking?' Then, depending on his answer, I'd say something like, 'Yep, you're on the right track there,' or 'Let's back up and look at that word. . .' I could tell he knew the material."

The test, which most students can do in three hours, took me six and a half long hours to complete. At the end, I was exhausted. But I passed.

Professor Tyree said some nice things about me. "JT knew he was responsible for that course. There are a lot of seniors who don't take responsibility. But JT radiated positivity, and a quiet confidence."

My final course grade was B minus.

● ● ●

Twenty-two years of undergoing 16 major surgeries; 18 years after entering preschool and discovering that the way my brain was wired didn't fit in with the conventional way of learning; 14 years after being told I would be illiterate for life; 13 years after I was asked to leave a prestigious private school; 12 years after suffering through an operation that could have left me paralyzed; a decade after moving to another state to embrace a new way to study and then creating a homeschool for three years; six years after participating in radical changes in the approach to learning differences in that same prestigious private school; and four years after graduating cum laude from that school—after two decades of my family's struggle and frustration and persistence and experimentation and resilience and determination and faith, after all that, I graduated from High Point University.

With a final GPA of 3.21.

My biggest cheerleaders, my Papi and Nani and my Pa and Ma, were there to see it on that muggy May 5, 2018, alongside Mom and Dad. My aunts and uncles and cousins couldn't come to North Carolina, but sent congratulations. Fritz and Anne Rector, Steve Tattum, and Ladi and Martina couldn't come either, but they sent wonderful cards. So did Grace and Chris Fenton, Donna Martin and Julie Martin Kelly, Sarah Kennedy Gilpin, other

Grosse Pointe friends, Dr. Healey, and many other Liggett people and friends. So did Rosemarie and Dan Offenhauer and other Denver connections. So many cards and emails!

Dr. Peña was having his own milestone at the same time in Denver, Colorado. He was being honored with an endowed chair at Children's Hospital Colorado where he practices medicine. I taped a video greeting expressing my gratitude to him[4] which was shown at the ceremonial dinner.

Under gray skies, my class of a thousand kids packed the Promenade in the center of campus and listened to the singer-actor-philanthropist Josh Groban tell us to not be afraid of fear and to never back away from challenges.

Dr. Qubein followed and said, "Everyone wants to live on top of the mountain, but all the happiness and growth occurs while you're climbing it. It's the journey that counts."

He called on us to achieve success in our own way and to be a light in the darkness. "You have learned about the art of the possible at High Point University. So, yes you can. You were created for a reason."

Then, the moment was here. One by one, we walked onto the stage, received our diplomas, shook hands with Dr. Qubein and with Mr. Groban, and got our photographs taken. I felt so relieved and accomplished. It had been a lifetime in the making and years of hard work. Finally!

And then they untethered the bald eagle.

It's a tradition at HPU. The eagle—a symbol of freedom and strength and pride—flies over every graduating class just before they're sent out into the world. A cry of joy rose from my classmates and their 10,000 family members and friends on the Promenade. It was an emotional experience to be surrounded by them. I was soaring.

● ● ●

Attending university took everything I had and demanded more. And it proved to me that I had more—more than I thought I had.

If you aren't facing something right now like that—whether it's a learning issue, a medical challenge, or just life—you will in the future. And you will learn, as I did, that there's more to you than you know!

As an acquaintance at High Point wrote Mom and Dad, "We rejoice in the miracle of graduation for JT and your whole family! I know it has been a long prayer-filled journey. What an amazing story!"

I believe God wants you to be certain of that. He knows everything about you and has great plans for you. He guided my family to Dr. Rector, Dr. Pena, Ladislav Lettovsky, Steve Tattum, and so many others; to Denver Academy, University Liggett School, and High Point University. He placed people in our lives to make it possible for me to be healthy, to read and write, to master skills, and to graduate. I believe God can guide you in the same way, no matter what hurdles you're facing, not matter what summits you want to reach.

With faith, you can untether yourself from whatever is holding you back, and you can soar.

EPILOGUE

Boundaries Don't Exist (Mt. Kilimanjaro)

You're off to great places! Today is your day!
Your mountain is waiting. So, get on your way!

— Dr. Seuss

Travel Day: October 3, 2018

"Oh no!"

Ladi stopped dead in his tracks. We had just arrived at Jomo Kenyatta International Airport from Heathrow and taken the shuttle to the terminal. After slogging through security, we were headed for our flight to Kilimanjaro International Airport.

"Our bags. They weren't checked at Denver all the way to Tanzania."

Ladi and his wife, Martina, and I were on our way to that East African country to climb Mt. Kilimanjaro. It had always been on my bucket list. Now that I had graduated from college I had the time to tackle it, and my friends Ladi and Martina were the perfect hiking partners.

Ladi shoved his backpack at me. "Here! You two run to the gate. I'll go back to baggage claim and get our bags!"

Stunned, Martina and I watched him sprint away.

Ladi has spent decades working in the airline industry. He's brilliant and logical. He has traveled the world. He knows how airports work. But, somehow he overlooked one detail when he made the travel arrangements to Kili.

As soon as we had set the dates to climb Kilimanjaro, Ladi used his many air miles to book our flights to Nairobi, a travel hub for East Africa. He couldn't use them for a flight from Nairobi to Kilimanjaro, though, so he waited to make those final plans until we had chosen our expedition guide and other details. We actually bought tickets for that last leg just days before departure—and Ladi forgot to make sure our bags followed us!

Our flight to Kilimanjaro Airport was scheduled to take off in 30 minutes.

Ladi jogged through the connecting portion of the airport—where technically he wasn't in Kenya—and re-approached the bright blue immigration and customs counters, which we had just walked by, feeling grateful we didn't need to stand in the long queues there.

Then he spotted a less-busy section labeled for diplomats. He caught the eye of a customs officer there.

"Sir! My companions and I are going to Tanzania. Our flight leaves in a half an hour, and our luggage from London is not checked through. It's coming off the flight now. Can you help me?"

The man said Ladi needed a visa to enter the baggage-claim area, which was in Kenya.

"How much is it?" said Ladi, reaching under his shirt for the wallet hanging from his neck.

"Twenty dollars US," the man said.

Ladi gave him a $20 bill. The man put it in his pocket and demanded Ladi's passport. Then he assigned a female airport employee to go with Ladi to retrieve the bags.

It had been 20 or 30 minutes since we had gotten off our 747 from England, but no bags had been unloaded yet. The clock was ticking!

Ladi paced and rubbed his arms and looked at his watch and sighed deeply. What if the bags did not show up? What if we miss our Kili flight?

Then, Ladi heard the mechanism of the baggage carousel start to rattle. He held his breath. Thump, thump, thump went suitcases and boxes and duffels down the chute to the clicking platform. Finally, he saw our three bags!

Each weighed 44 pounds, which meant he had to carry 132 pounds—and fast! He is a very fit man, but not big. He threw one on each shoulder and put the strap of the third on his forehead, balancing the bag on his back. He looked odd but it worked.

The woman who had been with him had disappeared so he jogged back toward customs. He had to push through lines of unhappy travelers going the opposite direction.

He reached the desk where he had "bought" a visa and handed over his passport. The customs agent was nowhere to be seen.

Ladi asked someone where the man had gone. No one knew.

Ladi began to feel panicky.

"Where is your visa?" another official demanded.

Ladi was starting to explain why he didn't have one when another agent, a woman, came out of a door behind the counter.

"Are you American?" she asked Ladi.

Thank goodness. The first customs agent had given the woman Ladi's passport, because his shift ended. Then he went home (with Ladi's $20)!

Ladi called me and started to trot, bags thumping him as he went. He reached the secured area. I met him there and grabbed the luggage to give Ladi a break. Whew!

We reached the gate, with five minutes to spare. Both of us were sweating.

Martina just rolled her eyes.

● ● ●

We already had our hiking boots on when we boarded our 10:28 a.m. MST flight from Denver to Miami. Talk about excited!

At 6 p.m. EST the eight-hour redeye to Heathrow Airport in Great Britain took off from Florida, and Ladi and Martina promptly fell asleep, but I was too excited.

I posted on my blog[1] and my Instagram account. A bunch of people commented right away. A lot asked to follow me up Kilimanjaro. (My Garmen GPS log entries would be live online.)

I finally slept. Then we woke up the next day in London! Ladi introduced me to English tea and some English food he liked: potato pancakes and a sausage-like thing called black pudding.[2] They tasted pretty good, but I'm glad now that I didn't know what was in the "pudding"!

Britain was one of his favorite places. He and Martina had lived there for three years after they left what was then Czechoslovakia[3] in the early 1990s.

Our flight to Nairobi was on a Boeing 747. That was a unique opportunity, because these super giant airliners are slowly being taken out of service. We were on the upper level. I slept for most of the flight, which was eight hours and 40 minutes long, and then woke up in Nairobi. (That's when we had the mad dash to the gate while Ladi found our luggage.)

Then, the last leg: the flight to Kilimanjaro!

283

We landed at Mount Kilimanjaro Airport just minutes before midnight, local time. We went through customs and found our ride to our hotel, the Ameg Lodge in the small town of Moshi. By the time we arrived, it was 3 a.m., and we had been traveling for 33 hours. Turns out it was good we got that sleep on the airplane from London to Nairobi, because we had to be up at 7 a.m.!

● ● ●

The journey of a thousand miles begins with one step.

— Lao Tzu

Day 1: October 4, 2018
Starting Location: Umbwe Gate
Starting Elevation: 5,382 feet
Ending Location: Umbwe Cave Camp
Ending Elevation: 9,356 feet
Elevation Gain: 3,974 feet
Hiking Distance: 6.8 miles

It's common for climbers to rest a day after arriving in Tanzania before beginning their trek up Mt. Kilimanjaro. After all, it's the highest point in Africa: 19,341 feet! But, we three were pretty well acclimatized from spending so much time in the mountains of Colorado.

Ladi wanted us to not lose that advantage. That meant we should not linger at low altitude (Moshi's elevation is only 3,000 feet). Instead we should start the hike the morning after we landed. He didn't have to convince me!

Our head guide, Simon Mtuy,[4] and the assistant guide, Manase Lyimo, met us at our hotel. All climbs up Kilimanjaro require permits issued by the government's park authority and must be led by licensed commercial guides.[5]

Both of these men, whom we came to love, spoke English and were highly trained and experienced. They were authoritative, but friendly.

Simon, a tall, lean man, has owned and operated his expedition company for two decades and had a spotless safety record. Manase, a little shorter and always smiling, had worked for him for years.

Simon also is an ultra-runner. In 2006 he broke the world record for the fastest unassisted ascent-descent of Kilimanjaro, running up and down in nine hours and 22 minutes! ("Unassisted" meant he had to carry all his water and supplies himself; no one helped him.)[6]

A simple dirt road led to the majestic 652-square-mile Mt. Kilimanjaro Park. Clouds opened up as our driver approached the park gate, and suddenly we saw the mountain!

"That is a rare sight from this location," said Simon, who was riding with us.

Floating in mist, it looked mysterious and remote. And immense.

Kilimanjaro—or Kili, which is how locals often refer to it—means "mountain of greatness." It is the world's largest free-standing mountain. It's actually a gigantic formation with three dormant volcanos: Shira, Mawenzi, and Kibo. Shira is the oldest. Mawenzi is a jagged rock spire. And Kibo is the highest peak, the destination of most Kilimanjaro climbers.

Kibo itself has three concentric craters. The outer crater rim rises to its highest elevation at Uhuru Peak. That's where we were headed!

Passing through the park entrance, we found a place where we could fill our water bottles and Camelbacks. Then we said hello to the rest of our team: 15 porters!

The porters were strong, hardworking people. Some spoke only Swahili; some spoke a little English. They carried everything we didn't, which included tents, food, water, even a portable toilet! Quite a few of them made double trips up and down the mountain to resupply the team's fresh food. Some went all the way up with us to the top and back. We came to respect them deeply.

Stashing their lunches in bags handmade out of a material like a sheet, the porters loaded up our supplies and started up the trail ahead of us. Meanwhile, we had to wait for our permit, a special waiver.

Under Simon's guidance, Ladi, Martina, and I were taking the Umbwe Route, the most difficult and least traveled choice of seven established ways up the mountain. And we were going to make a key change.

Most trips take seven or eight days up and down. We wanted to make it in four days, taking advantage of being acclimatized to 14,000 feet from our hikes in Colorado. To accomplish this, we were starting out on Umbwe and then cutting over to traverse what's known as the Western Breach.

There's a reason why you need special permission to climb the Western Breach. It is probably a good thing that I didn't know how demanding it was going to be. I think I would have gone anyway, but you never know.

We hung out by the tall wooden sign that marked the start of the Umbwe Route. Eventually, two park guys came buzzing up on a motorcycle. One of them handed Simon our special permit. It was 10:37 a.m., Tanzania time. Each of us had to sign it.

All the bags the porters were going to carry had to be weighed. The maximum allowed is 32 pounds. Then the porters sang a song as a way to give respect to the mountain we were about to climb. We started our trek just before noon.

I was so excited. After years of dreaming and months of preparation, we were finally under way!

Simon led off, and Manase came behind. The forest path immediately started to climb into a dense high-elevation rainforest. It was green, green, green, and there were flowers everywhere.

Then, half an hour into the hike, my stomach started acting up. I had to go to the bathroom right away. I didn't know why (I had skipped my treatments during travel, so that could be it) and I didn't know where! Plus, I had forgotten TP!

Man! *This is the first leg and I'm already sick!* I was upset. But, I had to deal with it!

Good thing I had no idea what I was going to face in a few days.

● ● ●

We formed a single file. The trail was straight up!

Sections were so steep you had to use tree roots for steps and handle bars. We saw colobus and blue monkeys in the trees, and they let us know they saw us, too. Noisy! We finally reached a spot where the porters had set up a lunch stop. There were even tables and chairs!

The head cook was named Christopher Agga, but he asked us to call him Kiplet. He served roast beef lunch meat, bread, all the trimmings, and fruit. It looked wonderful, but I didn't want to eat much. I had one piece of bread and two very small bananas. (All the bananas in Tanzania are very small.)

Then we got back on the trail. The path narrowed to a steep climb on a ridge. We used our hiking poles a lot. Three more hard hours, and then we reached our camp for the night: Umbwe Cave Camp. Our tents and the toilet were already set up.

I did a treatment lying on my back in my tent, hooking my solution by a carabiner to the top of the inside of the tent. It was my first experience doing a treatment like this. It turned out all right.[7]

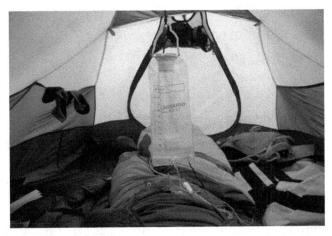

We had hiked nearly seven miles and climbed almost 4,000 feet on our first day. We had seen just one other hiker, a woman, during the entire time. The night was chilly, but nothing like what was coming.

● ● ●

We are tired, which is a good thing, since today's pain is tomorrow's strength.

— Ladislav Lettovsky

Day 2: October 5, 2018

Starting Location: Umbwe Cave Camp

Starting Elevation: 9,356 feet

Ending Location: Barranco Camp

Ending Elevation: 13,020 feet

Elevation Gain: 3,664 feet

Hiking distance: 3.9 miles

Among the people who live in the shadow of Kilimanjaro, there is a saying: "*Pole, pole.*" Pronounced "polay, polay," it is translated "slowly, slowly." But, it means a lot more than that.

When your guide says "*pole, pole,*" he's reminding you to follow a slow, steady pace that will help you conserve energy and avoid altitude sickness, so that you actually can make it to the summit.

But, the phrase has a broader, deeper meaning. It also means being present, listening, accepting, practicing patience, enjoying the moment. Above all, "*pole, pole*" is a way of life.

Ladi, Martina, and I were on the mountain, yes, to challenge ourselves physically and psychologically to climb up Uhuru Peak and back in four days (yes, the opposite of "slowly, slowly," but Ladi wanted us to spend as little time at the high altitude as possible).

But, just by being around Simon and Manase and the other team members, we also would end up learning about how to live the "pole, pole" way.

●　●　●

Day two on the Umbwe Route was shorter, but even steeper. The terrain was rockier, too, with sparser undergrowth. I felt good, but sore from the day before.

"Pole, pole," Manase reminded us, during a steep patch in the trail. "Go slowly."

That wasn't Ladi's style, though. For Ladi, "pole, pole" meant to pick a pace that he was comfortable with and then "zone in." He hiked alone and steadily, and took no breaks until he reached our next camp. That would be his custom until summit day.

Not only did he like to set his own speed, he also was leaving behind work-related stress. Walking ahead gave him time to be quiet with his thoughts. And since he was so experienced in mountains, he was confident he would have no problem keeping to the trail.

He had another motivation for walking separately. Martina and I had fallen into a rhythm, and Ladi didn't want to disrupt it.

"JT and Martina were connected hip-to-head, in tune with each other and with what was going on around them. They were immersed in their own world," he said after the trip.

We were having fun, Martina and me. We laughed and made the guides—Simon, Manase, and a guide-in-training named Robinson—smile, too.

These Tanzanians were very educated on everything about Kili, and we learned a lot. We had left behind the rainforest and entered the climate zone known as heath/moorland.[8] The path wound up through dense stands of strange, tall, straggly trees with trunks about the circumference of a can of beans. Hairy light-green moss hung from every branch, dangling over the trail like spider webs. Thicker moss on the ground was so soft and lush that our hands could sink into it six inches.

When the trail came up on to a slight ridge, we spotted Mt. Meru, 40 miles away, in a sea of thick clouds. It's Tanzania's second highest peak, and it was beautiful.

On this day we took rest stops along the way, but no formal lunch break. We carried snacks: organic granola bars and bites, trail mix, beef jerky, caramel chocolates, and candy-like chews made from electrolyte hydration drinks. I kept a stash in the pocket of my backpack's waist strap.

The shaggy trees gave way to others that looked like they were out of a Dr. Seuss children's book. These giant senecio plants looked like palm trees with succulents on top. They absorbed heat during the day and their wool-like insulation kept them warm through the freezing night.

The route became more like scrambling over rocks in a field of boulders. We reached the sheer, exposed Umbwe Ridge. We could see valleys and hear rushing water. Then we were overjoyed to see Mt. Kilimanjaro rising majestically on the horizon, all blue and white and beautiful. Very motivating!

Now we were on the rim of Barranco Valley, the location of our second camp. As a crossroads of most of the other routes up the mountain, Barranco is the busiest campsite on Kili. We descended and signed in. We asked our guides to pitch our tents in a secluded area and appreciated that the camp was quiet.

Barranco Valley was stunning, a giant bowl under the presence of the towering 843-foot-high Barranco Wall. I was amazed at the beauty. I could have enjoyed it for weeks. I felt close to God under the immense sky. Nature! I love it.

While waiting for Kiplet to prepare dinner, I wanted to let my parents know we had finished day two and were safe in camp. But, my phone had no connection. Neither did Martina's. Then we saw Ladi standing on a large rock above our tents. He had one bar! We gathered around the rock, put the phone in the middle on speaker, and called our families, letting them all know where we were. Not yet on top of the world, but getting there.

The sunset was incredible. Clouds gathered below and above us. The evening turned cold. The stars were mind-blowing! Photos can't do them justice.

Tomorrow, first thing, we would turn west and then north to climb 1,500 feet higher than my highest elevation experience, back on Mt. Elbert in Colorado. Then, things would get really challenging.

● ● ●

Believe you can and you're halfway there.

— Theodore Roosevelt

Day 3: October 6, 2018
Starting Location: Barranco Camp
Starting Elevation: 13,020 feet
Ending Location: Arrow Glacier Camp
Ending Elevation: 15,965 feet
Elevation Gain: 2,960 feet
Hiking distance: 2 miles

"JT?"

"JT!"

I heard Manase's voice outside my tent. It was still dark. I did not want to open my eyes, but our guides needed to "take our vitals," first thing. I sighed. Time to get up!

At least they offered us a hot beverage after the readings. Ladi and Martina always asked for coffee. I chose an herbal tea—a *Kilimanjaro*-brand one, of course.

"Taking our vitals" meant creating a baseline of our breathing rate and oxygen saturation. Manase counted our breathing. When we had started the hike, the rate per minute was probably around 16 breaths. As we got higher, it rose to 20, 30, and 40, until on the summit our bodies would be panting nonstop—sucking oxygen at 50 breaths per minute.

In addition, Manase read the level of oxygen saturation in our blood with an instrument called a pulse oximeter.

Clipped on the end of our fingers, the "pulse ox" uses infrared light to measure how red our blood was. (Blood cells that aren't carrying enough oxygen are bluer.) Normal rates are 95 to 100 percent.

Why was this important to do? Because, as the elevation got higher, there was less oxygen available in the air. If we didn't get enough O2, we might develop altitude sickness—which could range from feeling uncomfortable to becoming debilitated or even dying.[9]

You could take steps to help prevent altitude sickness. But, there was no way of knowing who would develop it and who wouldn't. People who are very fit can suffer, while people who are not fit might just as easily get by without any symptoms. Mountain-man Ladi, a former ultra-marathoner, had suffered badly for 24 hours when he climbed Argentina's Aconcagua, which at 22,841 feet is the highest mountain, not only in South America, but in all of the Americas. The customary climb is 20 days; Ladi summited and descended in nine.

The last time I had gone above an altitude I already had been at, I had gotten sick. How would I do today? And tomorrow—well, that would be almost 5,000 feet higher! How would my body react?

● ● ●

"JT, how are you?" Martina asked, as she did every morning. I'd gotten dressed and was outside, draping my parka and a few other items over the top of my tent to let them dry in the sun while we had breakfast. Condensation at night always got things damp.

"I'm good!" I said, as always. Better to be positive, right?

Martina and Ladi would laugh and later tell everyone that they decided early on that there were three levels of "I'm good."

"Level 1 was, Yes, JT is good. Level 2 was, 'I don't feel so good.' Level 3 was, 'Help!'" said Martina, who back home works as a registered nurse—something that soon was going to make a huge difference. "On this trip, we would see all levels on the mountain."

This morning I truly was good, and thankful. After a delicious meal of eggs, bacon, and fruit, we were being formally introduced to our porters, who were kind enough to entertain us with singing and dancing. Martina even got in the act![10]

Not all porters were men, by the way. We had two women, Maggie and Anna, among our group. I admired all of the porters very much. Their work was difficult and dangerous. Simon had a reputation for treating his employees well, but not all operations do. Often overloaded and underequipped, porters have died or been injured when it could have been avoided.

● ● ●

We broke camp and headed out around 9:30 a.m. It was pretty warm as we climbed along a river with waterfalls and rose from moorland terrain into the arid brown alpine desert.

Most hikers leaving Barranco Camp head south toward Karanga Camp and then Barafu Camp to circle around and approach Uhuru Peak from the south. We were going to climb in the opposite direction, past Lava Tower Camp and then north to Arrow Glacier—and the Western Breach.

A long series of multiple switchbacks made the climb nontechnical. There were only a few places where you had to scramble on all fours. The temperature dropped and we layered up. It took about an hour and a half to reach the ridge we were shooting for.

At that moment I glanced down at my altimeter that I kept hooked by carabiner to the shoulder strap of my daypack. It read 14,439 feet—the exact altitude I'd been at on Mt. Elbert![11] The highest I had ever been.

Our team took it slow, breathing steadily to keep our O2 levels high. Soon we were in mist. All you could see were the boulders you had to step around. Below us Lava Tower poked through. It was like walking on clouds.

"Hakuna matata!"[12]

I looked up. With mist swirling around him, Ladi was up on a massive cliff above us, feet spread, fists at his waist.

We laughed. "This guy thinks he can speak Swahili," said Simon, smiling.

Now we were close to the night's destination: the remote and infrequently used Arrow Glacier Camp at the foot of our next ascent: The foreboding and brutal Western Breach.

I was glad we were almost there, because I was starting to develop pressure in my head and a headache. I decided that it was likely that tomorrow I would experience some altitude sickness, and I had to prepare mentally for it. I would just have to keep fueled up and hydrated, go slow, and carry some Advil in my pocket.

There was no level ground anywhere. Rocks and glacier debris were strewn all over. The porters had positioned our tents close together. Mine was closest to the portable bathroom! Very kind!

Kiplet and his crew served us an afternoon snack of soup with noodles. It tasted so good. I did my treatment as soon as possible, before it got colder. It worked well.

I heard Ladi and Martina in their tent talking to my parents, so I jogged over and jumped on the call. It was something like 5:30 a.m. in Michigan. Mom and Dad sounded a little groggy. That's because they had been up all night watching my website, which had a live link to my Garmin GPS. Every 30 minutes, a little dot appeared on the digital topo map on their computer screen, marking our route and recording the elevation.

Then, I had to run to the bathroom! The results of my treatment hadn't gone the best. I felt off and a little bloated (sorry!). I didn't think it was related to the altitude, though. Tomorrow I'd feel better, I hoped!

After a yummy dinner, Simon told us to pack up as much as we could in preparation for tomorrow morning's early start. Very early, as in 4 a.m.!

Then he and Manase and Robinson passed out a new piece of equipment. There was no climbing the Western Breach without it: helmets.

As I burrowed into my sleeping bag it hit me. Tomorrow was it! The moment we'd been training and planning for. Summit day!

Would I make it?

• • •

Resilience can go an awful long way.
— Eddie the Eagle

Day 4: October 7, 2018

Starting Location: Arrow Glacier Camp
Starting Elevation: 16,029 feet
Highest Elevation: 19,359 feet—the Summit!
Ending Location: Mweka Camp
Ending Elevation: 12,750 feet
Elevation Gain: 3,330 feet
Elevation Change from Summit: 6,609 feet
Hiking distance: 1.8 miles

Imagine climbing the massive cone of a dead volcano. You feel about the size of an ant. Thick layers of ice coat the high rim, binding geological debris in place. At one point along its edge the crater has been notched— "breached"—by some ancient geological cataclysm. The mammoth fallout carved a wide, ragged chute down the slopes beneath the breach.

That's where you're heading.

Over eons of time—some experts say accelerated by global warming—the ice in the Western Breach has softened and receded. With that, the embedded material lodged in its crevices and outcroppings could suddenly become loose.

We're talking boulders the size of SUVs.

The resulting torrents of rock have maimed and killed dozens of climbers and porters. The latest reported death was an American in late 2015.[13]

The website for Simon's company states that, because of the danger, he no longer guides climbers up Kilimanjaro via the Western Breach Route.[14]

And yet, here we were, in single file behind Simon in the predawn darkness, heading up to the Roof of Africa—through the breach.[15]

● ● ●

When we woke at 4 a.m., ice coated the inside of our tents. The Kilimanjaro rain forest of two days ago seemed like a dream.

I felt pretty good. Yesterday's head pressure had gone away. We slipped on our headlamps and let Manase take our vitals. Our oxygen levels looked good to go. Breakfast was yummy hot oatmeal and raisins, full of iron, something our blood needed in this extreme elevation.

In the dim light we half-filled our bottles with cold water and then topped them off with hot water so they wouldn't freeze. Simon checked that we were wearing our helmets. Then, he went over our route with us while all but one of the porters left to descend for supplies. The remaining porter would ascend with us carrying emergency oxygen and medical equipment.

We departed Arrow Glacier Camp at 5:26 a.m. and headed east-southeast—and up.

Back home in Grosse Pointe, Michigan, it was 10:26 p.m. Two anxious parents were glued to my website, watching my Garmin GPS post a little dot every 30 minutes on the digital topo map, pinpointing our route and recording the elevation: 16,029 feet, 16,518 feet, 16,885 feet...

What the Garmin didn't tell Mom and Dad was how treacherous the climb was going to be. In all honesty, I didn't know either. Our headlamps lit up glacier silt, boulders stacked like gigantic bricks, and ice flows as we scrambled up the steep snowfields in the darkness.

One misstep and you could plummet several thousand feet.

Doing a route like this in the dark might seem crazy. But, it was crucial to cross the danger zone under the Western Breach before daybreak. Subfreezing temperatures meant a rockfall was less likely.

The stars were incredible. You felt as if you could reach up and touch a million points of light. Then, the sky began to slowly lighten. We stopped and leaned against gray boulders. Facing out and west, away from the mountainside, we gazed over a mammoth sea of thick clouds stretching 180 degrees to the horizon. The magnitude was breathtaking.

"Simon, is that Mt. Meru?" I asked. In the middle of the line where the puffy cloud bank met the pale sky was a large point, like a mountain peak shrouded by fog.

Simon chuckled. "No," he said. "That is Kili's shadow."

Mt. Kilimanjaro was behind us, and the sun was rising behind Mt. Kilimanjaro, casting a giant triangle over the land.

"There. That's Meru." Simon pointed to the left. Yes, I saw Mt. Meru then, poking up its nose in the vast expanse that was starting to glow with the rising sun.

We resumed climbing, stabbing the almost vertical rocky sides of the mountain with our hiking poles, then choosing each step among loose stones and debris. Sheets of ice streaked down like frozen fingers. We had to use our ice picks to create footing to cross them. There was no place to stop or even to stand; you had to lean into the mountain and keep traversing.

To look at where you had come from, you peeked under your stretched-out arm holding your hiking pole that you had thrust into the ground. Then, you sucked in your breath at the sight.

Thousands of feet down, and then a sheer drop.

We found an outcropping of boulders and rested. Then Simon caught our attention.

"My friends, we are at the point of no turning back."

From here on, Simon said, it would be too difficult to down-climb. We had made it across the funnel-like area notorious for falling rock. Now we were facing the Rock Steps. If evacuation became necessary, even if someone was suffering from life-threatening altitude sickness or had a broken leg or any other emergency situation, the only way out was up—hiking the five hundred more feet into the crater and then crossing it for a mile before being able to descend to the nearest (lower) camp for help.

I glanced at Ladi. Ladi was looking at Martina. Martina turned her gaze at me, and Ladi followed. We all smiled.

No way were we turning back now. Not after years of dreaming, months of training and planning, and four days of climbing! Not this close! No way!

But, in 15 minutes my confidence would be shaken.

Above us was what is called a false summit. From below, a false summit looks like the top of the mountain. You can't wait to get there. But, most often it's just another ridge with more terrain beyond it. We kept climbing.

That's when my stomach started to cramp with hot pain. It felt like it was boiling. A wave of nausea hit me. I pushed on. I didn't say anything to Martina or Ladi. But, it wasn't long before things got urgent. I knew I needed to find a place to use as a toilet, quick.

We were all standing for a moment, taking a breather.

"Martina," I said quietly, "I have a little stomach ache and have to go find—"

Just then we noticed that one of the porters who had gone for supplies was below us, returning with a heavy duffel bag. He had not taken the best route and was on a part of the icefield that was too high. If he fell, he could die.

We held our breath as the man slipped. He lost hold of his bag, but caught it in time and righted himself. Ladi turned to Simon and Manase.

"You guys have to go back and help him!" Ladi said. The man was risking his life for us.

Simon smiled and shook his head. If the porter truly needed assistance, he said, he or Manase would help. But, he had confidence the man was capable of handling his situation.

Ladi had to trust that Simon knew what he was talking about and was not being heartless. In a few hours we would see an example of how sacrificial Simon could be.

Meanwhile, I had a stunning view as I was taking care of business—which (sorry) was diarrhea. Now I knew my body was fighting a bug. I most likely had caught something, probably from untreated water, and because of my compromised intestinal system, I also was starting to feel signs of altitude sickness.

The summit was two hours away. Would I get so ill that Simon and Manase would have to carry me? Would I be unable to summit? Worse, would Ladi and Martina be forced to give up their own dream of summiting?

● ● ●

"When JT got sick on the mountain," recalls Martina, "He had two things to worry about. Altitude sickness and his intestinal issues. I was the most worried about dehydration. I had meds with me. I started him on antibiotics right away. I wanted to buy him some time, so he wouldn't miss the summit."

Martina had come equipped with a small cache of medical supplies. She later would say she regretted not bringing an IV with her, but that's getting ahead of the story. First, we had to reach Uhuru.

In the now-blinding sunlight, we finally crawled over the rocky Western Breach rim into Kibo's caldera. A stunning white mile-wide expanse met us. We started climbing a rock field up many ridges toward Kibo's wall-high Furtwängler Glacier, a remnant of an ice cap that once covered all of Kilimanjaro.

We paused for water and a snack, and a bunch of photographs. The wind was so fierce it was hard to stay upright. Simon encouraged us to get moving. He knew we were getting tired, and we had another hour to go.

That was just to the summit. We still had to descend as well!

As the three of us pushed on behind Simon, with Manase and the medical porter in the rear, the route started to zigzag over gravelly terrain up another ridge. I had to find another big rock, and that's when I threw up for the first time. It wouldn't be the last.

I started to realize I was getting weak. Ladi must have realized it too. He began "pacing" me—walking closely with me at a "pole, pole" pace so I could match his step and stay steady and focused.

Then it was 30 minutes to the summit. We couldn't see it yet, but I blindly pushed on, head down, trying to not think, trying to not feel. *Step. Breathe. Step. Breathe. Step. Breathe.*

The slope leveled out, and there 50 yards away, surrounded by 360 degrees of blue sky and anchored on a wide debris field, was the sign marking the summit!

Adrenaline kicked in! We started running.

"Give me the camera," panted Ladi. He began to videotape Martina and me.[16]

It was 11:28 local time. We had reached the summit in fewer than 72 hours since starting our climb.

(My poor folks had stayed up on and off all night. Later, they'd tell us they remember the moment they saw the live Garmin note that we'd reached 19,341 feet!)

I said thank you to Martina and hugged her, laughing. She said, No, thank you, JT. I hugged Ladi. I hugged Manase. I hugged Simon.

Just being up there made me think how amazing our God is. I'd never thought that I'd be able to do this! I felt so relieved, so happy. My sunglasses were fogging with hot tears.

"Simon, I'm so emotional. I'm crying! Thank you, thank you!"

"You're welcome. This is why I do this," Simon said, grinning. "I love helping people reach their goals!"

Then, photos. Lots of photos!

We three. Ladi and Martina. The whole team. Just me, and then me with a bunch of signs, such as a sign for Papi (for his upcoming 90th birthday) and a sign from my college alma mater, High Point University.

By then, we had been on Uhuru about 15 minutes. It was time to leave. It's not good for humans to be at that altitude for long, and we had a long way to go down. Besides, I had to throw up and go to the bathroom again!

● ● ●

The best view comes after the hardest climb.

— The Rockettes

Day 4: October 7, 2018
Starting Location: Arrow Glacier Camp
Starting Elevation: 16,029 feet
Highest Elevation: 19,359 feet—the Summit!
Ending Location: Mweka Camp
Ending Elevation: 10,138 feet
Elevation Gain: 3,330 feet
Elevation Change from Summit: 6,609 feet
Hiking distance: 11 miles

I so wanted to get off the mountain. Not because I didn't love being up there. We had set the goal of descending in one day. (Most treks take two or three days to go down.)

We could have done it. If I hadn't gotten sick.

"The dissent is brutal under the best of circumstances," remembers Martina. "It's difficult to hike down. It's hard on the joints, on the hips, on the knees and back. And then if you add sickness? That could destroy the experience. But, JT never complained."

What good would complaining do?

As soon as we made the decision to start down, we began jogging—actually, boulder-hopping, zig-zagging, sliding through scree. Down, down, down. We were in a hurry!

Our guide kept asking to carry my backpack. It's true I could have moved better without it, but I wanted to "carry my own weight," so to speak.

That started hours of seesaw suffering. I would feel okay, then I'd get nauseated and start to gag. I'd have to stop, sit or lie down, vomit, go to the bathroom, and rest a minute. Then, I'd feel better, resume jogging, be okay for a while, get nauseated, stop, throw up, et cetera, et cetera!

"Even when he was throwing up, he would finish and then he would smile at us," remembered Ladi. "I told him he needed to name this book chapter 'Throwing Up with a Smile!'"

We now knew for sure that on top of my stomach bug and the altitude sickness, I had become dehydrated. I just couldn't keep liquids down.

Ladi had told Martina, with her medical training, that she had the power to pull the plug on the plan to make it down the mountain all in one day. She watched me like a hawk.

"During that descent," recalls Martina, "when we were resting, I asked JT to stop drinking fluids, because it made him throw up more, and then he would lose more fluids. We regretted that we had no IVs."

We checked vitals. My oxygen level was 86 percent.

"His body wasn't getting enough oxygen. We had to get down. Rescue is very difficult on the mountain," said Martina. "Luckily the medication started to kick in, and he took a little food. I think things were a little safer, but I feared having to have him rescued."

● ● ●

Within 25 minutes of leaving Uhuru Peak, we came across something shocking.

A woman hiker was lying on her side off the trail, moaning. She was by herself, 400 feet from the summit. What had happened?!

Simon and Manase ran to her. Ladi and Martina came up behind. The poor woman, who we learned later was from Kenya, had fallen. Her leg was broken, and her shoulder dislocated.

The woman said her guide had left her there to take the rest of her group to the summit. Apparently, the trek was part of a fundraising effort. She said they assured her that they would come back for her, but still it was an awful thing to do. Simon frowned and shook his head.

"I will stay with her until they come," Simon volunteered. He always carried a satellite phone. There was no chance of calling in rescuers this high, but he could call ahead to the next available camp where she might be able to be picked up. Plus, he would help carry her down.

Manase led us down the mountain. Martina observed that the woman must not have been an experienced hiker. Perhaps she hadn't been able to train ahead of time.

"We had millions of places where we could have fallen, but didn't. Her group went through one challenging spot and she fell. That to me speaks to preparation," said Martina. "The 'team' of JT, Martina, and Ladi trained hard. There's a saying, 'Train hard, fight easy.'"

● ● ●

Still, as trained as we thought we were for this adventure, I was getting pretty wobbly. It was only midday, and we had thousands of feet to go in steep, rocky, scree-covered terrain.

"Ladi," said Martina. "No more. We're stopping at base camp."

She was referring not to the foot of Kili, but to Mweka Camp, which at 10,138 feet was still pretty high.

Ladi ran down ahead to talk to the porters at Mweka and explain my situation. They got a toilet ready, and set up our tents close together.

I was nearly crawling as we reached Mweka. My stomach hurt like heck. The pain, the dehydration, and the nausea all together made me feel the most miserable I've ever felt in my whole life. And there have been times when I've felt pretty miserable.

Martina agreed with my decision not to do a treatment, which might dehydrate me further. After an hour had gone by since I last threw up, she gave me some electrolytes. I kept them down and fell asleep.

I remember hearing Simon's voice outside my tent. I opened my eyes a little. It was dusk.

I heard Simon telling Ladi and Martina about the injured woman. He and others had carried her to the next camp and called for rescue. A helicopter had tried to reach her, but the cloud cover was too thick. She would have to stay on the mountain overnight.

I drifted off again.

"We got JT a throw-up bag," remembers Martina. "We could hear his air mattress squeaking as he threw up throughout the night."

It would be a tough night, but I was just grateful the rescuers didn't have to come for me.

● ● ●

"Never give in—never, never, never, never, in nothing great or small, large or petty, never give in except to convictions of honour and good sense."

— Winston Churchill

Day 5: October 8, 2018
Starting Location: Mweka Camp
Starting Elevation: 10,380 feet
Ending Location: Mweka Gate
Ending Elevation: 5,380 feet
Elevation Change: 5,000 feet
Hiking distance: 6.25 miles

The metal whack-whack-whack of helicopter blades passing overhead woke me up. It was early the next day, and the rescuers were going to make another attempt to reach the Kenyan woman.

Lying snug in my sleeping bag, I said a prayer for the poor lady, who likely was in more pain than I was.

"How is he?" I heard Simon's voice.

"JT! Time to get up!" Ladi belted out, laughing. I smiled. I was still very, very weak. But, I made myself unzip my tent flap and poke my head out.

"What's to eat?" I asked.

315

Martina just shook her head. "Oh you. Come on. Wash up first."

The wonderful porters had brought pans of warm water. We were filthy. Unlike the frozen trail up to the summit, the path down was super dusty. While our snow gaiters had kept our boots relatively clean, our hands, necks, and faces were coated.

In the camp's food tent, I managed two tiny bananas and a little bit of egg. Martina and Ladi were so hungry they ate the equivalent of two meals!

I took forever to pack. The porters were still breaking camp as we said goodbye to Mweka Camp and started walking, "pole, pole" style. They would soon pass us on the trail.

Half an hour into the very last leg of the descent, nature called. After I took care of that, we resumed walking, and 20 seconds later I had to go off trail again! That's the way it was most of the way down. At least two dozen stops. Not fun!

But, eventually there was nothing left, and even though I felt shaky, I was able to focus on getting down.

● ● ●

Martina had slowed, too. An old hip injury from last year was giving her trouble. Simon and Ladi stayed by her side. Manase and I would pull ahead, and then we would stop and let them catch up.

I noticed that Manase had tied a plastic bag to his backpack. When he saw trash along the path, he would pick it up. The trail was heavily traveled by climbing teams. Protein bar wrappers, sports drink bottles, old bandages, all sorts of garbage littered the route.

"This is our mountain," Manase said, smiling. "I want to respect it."

That motivated us all to pick up litter too. Ladi said he was going to make it a practice from this point on all his hiking adventures.

We were in the rain forest now. One time while Manase and I were waiting, I heard monkeys screeching overhead. Manase moved a few feet to the left and motioned for me to do the same. Drops of liquid began to hit tree leaves and then the dirt.

"They're peeing on us!" I laughed. We moved again, and so did the monkeys. I guess they were like dogs, "marking" their territory.

Finally, there was Mweka Gate.

We were down.

Manase came up behind me, and in a few minutes, Simon, Ladi, and Martina stomped into sight.

I was grinning ear to ear. So relieved and grateful! We had made it!

● ● ●

I called my parents. It was 7:02 a.m. in Michigan. They were groggy, but happy.

That's when I finally let them know I'd been sick from before the summit. They were so happy I was down!

We all signed out of the park.

Goodbye for now, Kili!

Our walking wasn't over, though. We had another mile to go to where we would have our final meal with our team and say goodbye to the porters.

Our destination actually was Simon's family farm. Simon leased a beautiful place, which lay along the park boundary. (All land in Tanzania is owned by the government, which then can lease it to private citizens for up to 99 years.) It was not only where he and his family lived. It was where he had a large farm operation using complex and productive sustainable farming practices known as permaculture.

All the food we were served was fresh from the farm. I ate only a banana and a meat-filled pastry of some sort, because I didn't know how my system would react and I wasn't feeling great. But, there were delicious-looking sliced pineapples and citrus, and the stuffed avocados were the size of small melons.

The goodbye ceremony with all the guides, cooks, and porters was wonderful. There was a lot of singing and dancing. Simon gave each of us a certificate verifying that we had made it to the top of Kilimanjaro.

Then we had to say goodbye to these people we respected and had relied on, who risked their lives to keep us alive. "We truly bonded with them in the camps," said Martina. It was bittersweet.

● ● ●

Life begins at the end of your comfort zone.

— Neale Donald Walsch

Post-Climb Days

We would be back the next day for a tour of the family farm. For now, a hired driver was going to take us on a two-hour trip to the other side of the mountain. The location was another farm, the one on which Simon had grown up.

Simon had built a little hotel there for climbers on his expeditions, so they could stay there for a day or two to get acclimated. It consisted of rustic small wooden bungalows connected by decks and walkways lined with log rails. That's where we would be sleeping.

On the way, Martina and Ladi asked to stop in town. They had their hearts set on bringing home some tanzanite, a beautiful dark blue gemstone that can only be found in Tanzania.

By the time we reached our destination, it was dark. The path to the hotel was uphill and not accessible by vehicle. So, we put on our headlamps and backpacks and started hiking again!

We didn't know any of the people on the farm or at the hotel, but they were very friendly. We were the only guests. They fed us and showed us our clean, cheerful bedrooms. They had real toilets and a real shower! Luxurious!

I did my treatment and went to sleep in a real bed. Boy, did that feel good!

● ● ●

The next morning, we heard kids playing outside the window. Someone pointed out the house Simon had grown up in. He had instructed us to take it easy, and asked his manager to give us a tour of the farm and the surrounding ones.

So, we practiced "pole, pole," meandering and soaking everything in. We saw fields, streams, and waterfalls.

We learned how to grow and harvest coffee beans; we even shelled, roasted, and brewed some coffee!

We encountered some women who lived nearby and talked with them. They were carrying tree logs and giant bundles on their heads. Amazing strength. We all tried it and flinched!

The next morning we went back to Simon's family farm and spent the day there. I think all of us were so blown away by all that we learned there that it almost rivaled our time on Kilimanjaro. But, that's another story!

The flight home was uneventful. (Thankfully!) After we got back, we all three said it would take weeks or maybe months to process our experiences. I'm still working on that!

One thing that Kilimanjaro taught me for sure: Mountains are for climbing.

In other words, *slow, steady steps over any hurdle you face will bring you victory.*

I don't remember saying this, but Martina swears it happened.

"At the very end, what did both JT and Ladi say? 'What's *next?!'*"

Martina laughed. "Holy smoke!

A FINAL WORD

I want to encourage you.

I've gone through so much already in my life that I'm confident that whatever you're facing right now, you can overcome it.

Not just overcome it. You can achieve great things!

If you untether!

You have the power to make things happen. If you don't have a lot of resources around you, go find them! You'll be surprised by what doors you can open, just by knocking—courteously, but persistently!

Yes, always be kind. Always think of others.

You don't know what people are going through.

Look for ways to help them. That boosts them up, but it also can bring you joy.

I believe faith and a positive attitude are everything.

The God who created you loves You!

You can trust that every day Jesus is helping you create a life full of purpose.

It may not look like you thought it would. But, it can be full of joy and laughter and accomplishments and fulfillment!

So, never, never, never give up!

Untether!

I'd love to pray for you!

Feel free to write me at JTMestdagh.com

— JT

END NOTES

Chapter 2

[1] A child with TEF often also suffers from esophageal astresia. It occurs when the esophagus does not fully form and there is no connection between the mouth to the stomach.
https://www.cincinnatichildrens.org/health/t/trach-fistular

[2] With anal atresia or an imperforated anus, the rectum and the anus did not develop properly. The anus may be covered by a membrane, or not exist at all. Often, the condition exists along with other anorectal malformations.
https://www.cincinnatichildrens.org/health/a/anorectal-malformations

[3] Approximately 50 percent of babies with anorectal malformations like I had have other abnormalities. These commonly include:

- Spinal abnormalities, such as hemivertebra, absent vertebra and tethered spinal cord

- Kidney and urinary tract malformations, such as vesicoureteral reflux, horseshoe kidney and duplication of parts of the urinary tract

- Congenital heart defects

- Tracheal and esophageal defects and disorders

- Limb (particularly forearm) defects

- Down syndrome, Hirschsprung's disease, and duodenal atresia may also be seen with anorectal malformation

https://youtu.be/iLwIVYDwGCY

[4] https://youtu.be/RpLNaARmO5U

[5] VATER association (pronounced "vah-ter") is actually a bunch of birth defects. Some can be life threatening. Some are more just annoying. We'll learn more about it in the chapters to come.

Chapter 3

[1] "Post-lumbar puncture headaches" have been described as "a headache like no other."

[2] When creating a double-barrel colostomy, the surgeon divides the bowel completely. Each opening is brought to the surface as a separate stoma. One stoma puts out stool; one is inactive. Waste comes whenever the body decides it need to eliminate. There's no warning.

These links give you an idea of what my parents (and families like them) had to deal with:

https://handtohold.org/10-tips-for-your-babys-colostomy-care

https://www.youtube.com/watch?v=i__eMqi76f0

http://www.preemiebabies101.com/10-tips-for-your-babys-colostomy-care/

[3] Ostomy refers to the actual surgery that changes (temporarily or permanently) the way waste exits the body. http://www.ostomy.org/What_is_an_Ostomy.html

[4] Sarah Kennedy is now Sarah Gilpin. She and her husband, James, have a sweet daughter who also takes a little extra care, because of being born with diabetes.

Chapter 4

[1] The surgery was for bilateral inguinal hernias. A hernia is an unwanted opening in the wall of abdominal muscle, allowing tissue to bulge out. Inguinal means in the groin area. Bilateral here means

on both sides of the body. Most inguinal hernias happen, because an opening in the muscle wall does not close as it should before birth.

[2] https://ghr.nlm.nih.gov/condition/vacterl-association. The newer term VACTERL is an acronym with each letter representing the first letter of one of the more common malformations seen in affected children:

(V) = (costo-) vertebral abnormalities

(A) = anal atresia

(C) = cardiac (heart) defects

(TE) = tracheal-esophageal abnormalities, including atresia, stenosis, and fistula

(R) = renal (kidney) and radial abnormalities

(L) = (non-radial) limb abnormalities

(S) = single umbilical artery

[3] https://ghr.nlm.nih.gov/condition/vacterl-association

https://www.ncbi.nlm.nih.gov/pmc/articles/PMC3169446

http://www.tofs.org.uk/vacterl-an-overview.aspx

https://rarediseases.org/rare-diseases/vacterl-association

[4] Posterior is the location of the surgery (here meaning from the back). Sagittal has to do with the imaginary vertical midline of the body. Anorectoplasty is surgery that repairs defects of the rectum and/or anus.

[5] https://www.childrenscolorado.org/doctors-and-departments/departments/colorectal/colorectal-procedures; https://www.youtube.com/watch?v=s49vpN4WGM8; https://bit.ly/2NCYmTw

[6] https://www.childrenscolorado.org/doctors-and-departments/departments/colorectal/colorectal-procedures/

https://www.childrenscolorado.org/doctors-and-departments/departments/colorectal/colorectal-procedures/anal-dilation

Chapter 5

[1] Think of the way an earthworm propels itself. That's the motion created by peristalsis, where smooth muscle tissue moves a substance along. In the gastrointestinal tract (esophagus to anus), peristalsis moves food and waste from mouth to anus in waves. For unknown reasons, I had no peristaltic muscles, and had to sit up and rely on liquids and gravity to make the system work. Sometimes it didn't.

Chapter 6

[1] "Motility" is the coordinated movement of the colon to help push poop toward the body's exit. At this point, we didn't know I didn't have normal motility.

[2] Megacolon is a condition in which the colon is abnormally dilated (stretched out) due to the accumulation of stool. In children, megacolon can be caused by several underlying conditions including Hirschprung's disease and severe constipation. An untreated megacolon can lead to serious complications.

[3] Biliary atresia is a rare disorder of the liver and bile ducts. Cells within the liver produce liquid called bile, which carries waste products to the intestines for excretion. This network is called the biliary system. When a baby has biliary atresia, bile gets trapped inside the liver, causing and eventually liver failure; https://www.cincinnatichildrens.org/health/b/biliary

Dr. Pena wrote that the short life of his first son, Gustavo, "will always be a major factor to explain my career." (*Monologues of a Pediatric Surgeon* (Amazon Digital Services, 2011) ebook p. 346).

[4] https://www.childrenscolorado.org/doctors-and-departments/departments/colorectal/colorectal-procedures/bowel-management/

Chapter 7
_____

[1] David Saltzman, *The Jester Has Lost His Jingle* (The Jester Co. ,1995). Saltzman wrote and illustrated the book as his senior project at Yale University before his death from Hodgkin's disease in 1990; http://www.thejester.org.

In a moving Afterword, Maurice Sendak, the author-artist of *Where the Wild Things Are*, wrote that David "managed through his harrowing ordeal to produce a picture book so brimming with promise and strength, so full of high spirits, sheer courage and humor is nothing short of a miracle . . . David's Jester soars with life."

[2] https://www.rmhc.org.

Chapter 8
_____

[1] Giardia is a common microscopic waterborne parasite that causes the illness known as giardiasis. It's associated with "catching" it near water sources like lakes and rivers, but it can be present anywhere, even municipal water supply. The symptoms often are abdominal cramps, bloating, nausea, and diarrhea.

http://www.mayoclinic.org/diseases-conditions/giardia-infection/basics/definition/con-20024686

Chapter 9
_____

[1] From March 3, 2003: Psycho-educational evaluation, Marquita Bedway, psychologist

[2] https://www.nimh.nih.gov/health/publications/attention-deficit-hyperactivity-disorder-adhd-the-basics/index.shtml; https://www.additudemag.com/slideshows/add-vs-adhd/

[3] https://sites.ed.gov/idea; https://www.ncld.org/archives/action-center/learn-the-law/individuals-with-disabilities-education-act-idea

Chapter 11

[1] "Happy Birthday, Jesus," composed by Carol Cymbala.

Chapter 13

[1] https://rarediseases.info.nih.gov/diseases/4018/tethered-cord-syndrome; https://www.ninds.nih.gov/Disorders/All-Disorders/Tethered-Spinal-Cord-Syndrome-Information-Page

Chapter 14

[1] The human body is so interconnected that damage to one area affects many areas. In this case, the signals between the brain and the bladder via my increasingly compromised spinal cord suddenly weren't getting through.

Chapter 15

[1] The spine runs from the skull to the pelvis. It has 33 wing-like bones termed vertebrae, which are divided into four regions: cervical, thoracic, lumbar, and sacrum.

https://www.spineuniverse.com/anatomy/vertebral-column

Chapter 17

[1] The Mitrofanoff Catheterizable Stoma would allow me to catheterize myself, reducing accidents. It's similar to the Malone procedure, which you'll learn about in chapter 24.

[2] Tattum F.A.S.T. Reading is the name of Stephan Tattum's program in Michigan, where it has been well researched and gained wide

usage in school districts, private institutions, and homeschool, afterschool, and tutoring programs. (F.A.S.T.= Foundations of Analysis, Synthesis, and Translation.) Nationally, the program is referred to as Tattum Reading. Learn more at www.tattumreading.com. Tattum also has partnered with other programs, such as Beyond Basics (in Detroit), and has created new learning centers in the Bay Area in Northern California called LearnUp Centers (learnupcenters.org).

Chapter 18

[1] It's all about "firing" the right part of the brain. Watch this amateur video that captures Steve in an educator training session giving an overview of the process the brain uses to learn words : https://www.youtube.com/watch?v=joafnpBR5iA

[2] Steve says that in his many years of working with nonreaders or kids with learning differences, he repeatedly notices that children usually "take off" their "mask" within a month or two of working with his reading program. "Parents will comment that the child I knew at age 5 has returned!" he says.

Chapter 19

[1] http://bethesda.fallshosting.com/history

[2] Mrs. Friend, who is now Mrs. Knightcap, wrote this nice note about our time at Denver Academy.

In my work with children with learning disabilities, there is often much work to be done to restore their self-esteem and restructure their belief about themselves before you can make true progress. Setbacks can be numerous and devastating for a child with learning differences. However, in JT's case, he didn't deny or ignore having experienced setbacks and obstacles, but he did not allow them to overpower his resilient spirit. He simply put his setbacks aside and focused his attention on progressing forward—which he did!

Frankly, I have never had a student like JT. I've thought of him over the years as a symbol of what can be accomplished when you don't waste time clinging to your worries or possible disadvantages, but instead, remain unwaveringly optimistic and *patiently trusting the process. This skill of his illustrated a wisdom that is quite rare in children and clearly served him well on his path to happiness and achievement.*

Chapter 21

[1] You can gain more information about Steve's program by visiting www.tattumreading.com. He also gives a thorough overview as a guest in December 2016 on the online show, "This Is America with Dennis Wholey": https://www.youtube.com/watch?v=RAKwi4l3h54

Chapter 22

[1] This is what Mrs. Vreede wrote my mother:

I have always been so very impressed and taken note of JT's commitment to speak to every training class, his confidence in standing before groups large and small, expert and not, as Steve throws various curve balls his way, and his courage to read aloud and be pushed for speed and accuracy, again in front of audiences filled with educators, parents, administrators, students, and more. JT is always so courteous, kind, dedicated, determined, such a great listener and always responds with positivity. And all the while, he lets me take his picture!

[2] A five-year study found that implementation of the F.A.S.T. Reading program was "significantly successful," as well as cost effective (averaging $186 per pupil). A professor at Easter Michigan University, working with the superintendent of Grosse Pointe Public School System and a district math teacher, studied data from five years (2007-2012) of reading results. (See "Implementation of a Reading Intervention Program: Internal Assessment and Cost Benefit Analysis," By Derek R. Fries, Eastern Michigan University, Tom Harwood, and Greg Johnson, Grosse Pointe Public School System, in *Michigan Reading Journal* 2014 (Vol. 47, No. 1) pp. 28-35.)

A summary is here:

www.tattumreading.com/uploads/1/3/2/1/13211620/grosse_pointe _study.pdf

In "Making F.A.S.T. Readers," Kelly Mozena, Grosse Pointe Magazine, September-October 2014, GPPSS superintendent Thomas Harwood called the program "a wonderful learning opportunity"; and Dr. Fries was quoted as reporting the following gain in reading test scores: "Children who used F.A.S.T. experienced a 23 percent increase in MEAP scores and a 52 percent increase in NWEA scores" (p. 18).

Chapter 23

[1] Here's one of Mrs. Dettlinger's recollections:

> "A celebration of the teacher becoming the learner and the learner becoming the teacher, was when I was working with JT the summer between fifth grade and sixth grade. . . Kris had reached out to me to see if I was interested in working with J.T. with FAST when Steve was [not in town]. Any chance to work with JT is a pleasure.

> Since I was just learning F.A.S.T. I jumped at this opportunity. I had only been trained in the [previous] fall and since I worked with first graders I was only really knowledgeable with the beginning concepts. I could go over the board with JT and follow the book to review and reinforce concepts but the pieces beyond that JT taught me.

> He had a system of what came first, second, and third and easily moved from one skill to the next without having to look up anything. If I ever looked at the manual for guidance, he was right. He was a whiz at timed readings, logging and recording data, and the use of the Words and Quotes book. He approached our hour-long sessions with seriousness and focus; those same traits I saw back when he was six.

> This internal motivation and never ever-quit attitude has been huge for JT's success and will continue to attribute to his success. He believes he can do anything and he has been able to do just that!

Chapter 24

[1] https://www.webmd.com/digestive-disorders/picture-of-the-appendix

[2] Long medical names make it easy to see why we shorten them! The appendicostomy known as the Malone is an antegrade ("from above") continence enema procedure—meaning it allows patients to give themselves an enema while sitting on the toilet, rather through the rectum.
https://en.wikipedia.org/wiki/Malone_antegrade_continence_enema

Chapter 25

[1] The falls (there are five all in a line) aren't the widest or tallest in the world. But cumulatively, the Victoria Falls produce the biggest curtain of falling water. (www.victoriafalls-guide.net/largest-waterfall.html). That qualified them for being on the list of the Seven Natural Wonders of the World (sevennaturalwonders.org), which includes the Aurora Borealis, the Harbor of Rio de Janeiro, the Grand Canyon, the Great Barrier Reef of Australia, Mount Everest, and Paricutin, a volcano in Mexico.

Chapter 27

[1] Because of our bond, Dr. Reddy and I had appointments into my early 20s, even though he is a *pediatric* urologist. We had frank talks as I got older, include a "man-to-man" discussion of how my condition might impact all aspects of life, including sexuality. He reminded me questions about such issues are nothing to be ashamed of; everyone wonders, and should feel open and free to bring it up with their health providers.

[2] *Cura personalis* is a centuries-old key teaching of the Society of Jesus, a Roman Catholic order also known as the Jesuits. It conveys a spiritual principle that individuals are worthy of our caring about their needs as whole people (social, emotional, spiritual, as well as physical and medical). Knowing that families trust their children to him and his colleagues, Dr. Reddy— as director of the division of pediatric urology—instituted this approach throughout the department.

Chapter 28

[1] According to the state Geological Survey. Alaska is in second place with 29, 22 of them the highest; California has 12, and Washington, two. (See www.14ers.com)

[2] Mount of the Holy Cross might be Colorado's most famous mountain. A deep couloir on the face of the peak is intersected by a ledge and gets filled with snow, making—you guessed it—a cross. Before photography, the cross was rumored to exist but not many had seen it. In August 1873, the photographer William Henry Jackson set out to prove its existence by taking a picture of it. His black-and-white photograph became famous, and drew Christian pilgrims into the first part of the next century.

[3] vailmountainrescue.org

[4] https://www.climbing.com/skills/learn-this-laws-of-lightning/

[5] Michelle Vanek was last seen on September 24, 2005 (www.denverpost.com/2005/12/03/missing-hikers-trail-littered-with-questions). James Nelson went missing October 2010 (www.denverpost.com/2013/10/10/eagle-county-coroner-skull-is-that-of-chicago-hiker-missing-since-2010).

[6] Backcountry travelers should always carry the "10 Essentials," including extra clothing, food and water, in case they run into trouble (www.mountaineers.org/blog/what-are-the-ten-essentials.)

[7] www.fs.usda.gov/recarea/whiteriver/recarea/?recid=41405

[8] The Notch Mountain Shelter was built in 1933 as a shelter for Holy Cross pilgrims (coloradoencyclopedia.org/article/notch-mountain-shelter).

[9] After the climb, Papi and Nani, Mom and Dad, and I visited a Vail Mountain Rescue (VMR) meeting. Dominik was there too, with his father. They gave Dominik and me a plaque for completing the Halo Route! Later, Papi and Nani made a donation to VMR for an indoor climbing wall for search-and-rescue training. We were surprised to learn that the wall is named "JT's and Dominik's wall."

Chapter 29

[1] Assistive educational technology is any aid or device that helps a person learn, whether it's dictation software, audio players, recorders, timers, smartphones, grammar checkers, text-to-speech software, and so on.

[2] Cum laude in Latin means "with great praise." The phrase usually is used to describe a graduation "with honor" or "with distinction."

Chapter 30

[1] http://www.nidoqubein.com.

[2] http://www.highpoint.edu/academicservices/learningexcellence.

[3] http://www.highpoint.edu/oars/

[4] https://vimeo.com/329462469

EPILOGUE: Boundaries Don't Exist (Mt. Kilimanjaro)

[1] http://www.jtmestdagh.com/blog

[2] Black pudding is a sausage-like item made from pork blood, along with animal fat and some sort of cereal, usually oatmeal, oat groats, or barley groats.

[3] Communist Czechoslovakia split into the Czech Republic (now also known as Czechia) and Slovakia in 1993.

[4] Simon Peter Mtuy is founder of Summit Expeditions & Nomadic Experiences(www.nomadicexperience.com).

[5] www.tanzaniaparks.go.tz/index.php/2016-01-30-07-32-00/2016-01-30-07-45-26/2016-01-30-07-47-52

[6] http://www.climbmountkilimanjaro.com/about-the-mountain/record-climbs; http://www.youtube.com/watch?v=VD_GmsyQS_I

[7] https://vimeo.com/329468588

8 The five climate zones on Kili are savannah/bush land (which is at the foot of the mountain, so not truly on the climb); rain forest; heather / moorland; alpine desert; arctic (https://earthobservatory.nasa.gov/images/89605/the-zones-of-kilimanjaro).

9 http://www.altitude.org

10 https://vimeo.com/329483916

11 Ladi and Martina and I actually had tackled Mt. Elbert during our pre-Kili training. Before we reached its summit, Ladi had split off to go hunting. His hidden agenda was to make Martina and I have to camp in the dark by ourselves. We froze, but it was great practice—experiencing the elevation, enduring the environment, and developing trust!)

12 A Swahili phrase meaning "No worries," made famous by the 1994 movie, "The Lion King."

13 A January 2006 rock fall killed three American climbers and injured another climber and four porters. In September 2015, an American man was killed and others injured, as well.

14 I later asked Simon about his decision to state on his website that he and his guides don't lead climbers to the summit via the Western Breach (WB) route. Here's how he replied:

> "We don't want to take too much risk for WB. However, [we will consider] clients that [understand] the mountain and the risk. And, of course we need to have good guides who can make clear decisions, etc."

Then I asked him how he decided to make an exception for Ladi, Martina, and me. He wrote,

> "I knew that you and Ladi know us very well, and if we have [to] make any changes, that will be easy. And, of course you are fully aware of the mountain and risk!"

15 "I'm always apprehensive on steep climbs," recalls Ladi. "A rockfall was definitely a real probability on this approach. But, Simon was

able to obtain the special permit needed, because his team has a spotless safety record."

[16] https://vimeo.com/329474621

APPENDIX A:

A Brief List of Medical Related Information

Hospital Centers / Resources

• International Center for Colorectal and Urogenital Care
at Children's Hospital Colorado (in Aurora, Colorado, near Denver)

Alberto Pena, MD, Director; Andrea Bischoff, MD, Assistant Director.
www.childrenscolorado.org/doctors-and-
departments/departments/colorectal/
Facebook: Doctors Pena Bischoff@doctorspenabischoff.

Facebook: Colorectal Support Network

Twitter: DoctorsPenaBischoff@DrsPenaBischoff

Instagram Drs Peña and Bischoff@penabischoff

• Regarding the need for care as children with malformations
become adults:

www.childrenscolorado.org/doctors-and-

departments/departments/urology/programs-clinics/transitional-

urology/

• The Colorectal Center
at Cincinnati Children's Hospital Medical Center

(Founded by Dr. Alberto Pena before he moved to Children's
Hospital Colorado)

www.cincinnatichildrens.org/service/c/colorectal

VATER/VACTERL Information

• VATER Syndrome/VACTERL Association Information
on the Cincinnati Children's Hospital website

Includes a glossary, causes, related health problems,

www.cincinnatichildrens.org/health/v/vacterl

- "VACTERL association," *Genetics Home Reference, National Library of Medicine,* which is part of the National Institutes of Health, an agency of the U.S. Department of Health and Human Services. Provides an overview and discusses frequency, diagnosis, treatment and other questions.
ghr.nlm.nih.gov/condition/vacterl-association

Support Organizations

- *TOFS (Tracheo-Oesophageal Fistula Support)*

An association maintained in Great Britain, TOFS is a website packed with free information and support.

- *Pull Thru Network*

A website-based volunteer non-profit organization dedicated to providing information, education, support, and advocacy for families, children, teens, and adults who are living with the challenges of congenital anorectal, colorectal, and/or urogenital disorders, and any of the associated diagnoses. The website is a wealth of support, information, and resources. www.pullthrunetwork.org

Lending a Hand to Increase Awareness of Colorectal Congenital Problems

Dr. Pena and Dr. Bischoff have mounted a social media campaign to raise awareness of congenital colorectal problems. They've devised a simple symbol using an open left hand (for "rare disease") and a fist (for "fight"), placed over the person's lower back.

Machu Picchu, Peru, June 2018.

This is a letter from Dr. Peña to my parents.

From: Pena, Alberto
To: Kristine B. Mestdagh
Sent: Mon, Feb 27, 2017 10:44 am
Subject: RE: J.T. Mestdagh 9-13-95

Dear Mr. and Mrs. Mestdagh:

It is great to hear from you and to learn that J.T. is doing well in college. Please tell him that we are proud of him. I take this opportunity to ask you to accept my admiration and respect for your dedication and love and all what you have done for him. I must tell you that J.T. is a special human being. Ever since I remember him, he has been smiling; he seems to be always happy and transmits that happiness to those who surround him.

In casual, informal conversations with friends and relatives, talking about what we expect from our children, most parents expect great achievements from their children. Of course, that is highly desirable. However, I have a different opinion, based on my experience through life. I prefer to have a happy son or daughter, without diplomas and degrees, rather than a depressed PhD or a genius with "existential problems", trying to "find himself", or with addiction problems.

As you know, Andrea [Bischoff, Dr. Pena's wife and a fellow physician] and I have been in contact with thousands of patients suffering from different types of congenital conditions, with different degrees of severity. We have been trying to follow them as long as possible and by doing that we have learned a lot about the different ways in which human beings deal with adversity.

Some patients with minor defects suffer a lot and blame on their defect for all that goes wrong in their life; they almost become social handicapped individuals.

On the other hand, we see other admirable individuals, suffering from much more serious problems, and yet they take a positive, optimistic attitude, learn to deal with their limitation and even go further to help others. I think J.T. belongs to this last category and the project of the book confirms my idea.

Alberto Peña, MD, FAAP, FACS, FRCS | Director, International Center for Colorectal Care| Children's Hospital Colorado| Professor of Surgery University of Colorado

13123 East 16th Avenue, Box 323 | Anschutz Medical Campus | Aurora, CO 80045

Phone: (720) 777-9988| Fax: (720) 777-7891 | Alberto.Pena@Childrenscolorado.org

Connect with Children's Hospital Colorado on Facebook and Twitter

Children's Hospital Colorado
International Center for
Colorectal Care

APPENDIX B:

Learning Differences

Tattum Reading System

- *Tattum Reading*

  Stephan Tattum's ground-breaking reading program is a synthesis of whole language and phonetic instructional techniques designed to help students break the phonetic code while involving them in meaningful reading and writing from the first day in the program.

  www.tattumreading.com

- *Tattum F.A.S.T. Reading*

  This is the name of the program in Michigan, where it has been well researched and gained prominence. Nationally, the program is referred to as Tattum Reading.

  (F.A.S.T. is an acronym for Foundations of Analysis, Synthesis and Translation, the three actions for the brain during reading.)

- *LearnUp Centers*

  This is a growing new endeavor in the Bay Area of Northern California. Steve Tattum and a staff of tutors use Tattum Reading structure and materials in stand-alone centers. The website has a wealth of information available.

  learnupcenters.org

Expert Resources

Brooke and Jennette Eide, *The Dyslexic Advantage: Unlocking the Hidden Potential of the Dyslexic Brain* (Plume, 2012)

Ben Foss, *The Dyslexia Empowerment Plan: A Blueprint for Renewing Your Child's Confidence and Love of Learning* (Ballantine, 2016)

Dr. Sally Shaywitz, *Overcoming Dyslexia: A New and Complete Science-Based Program for Reading Problems at Any Level* (Vintage, 2005)

Support Organizations

• *International Dyslexia Association*

Promotion of evidence-based research into dyslexia, and into how to teach people with dyslexia and how to train teachers to teach them. Offers extensive resources for families, educators, administrators, educational psychologists and counselors, and people with dyslexia.

https://dyslexiaida.org/

• *Learning Disabilities Association of America*

Offers information, education, school support, and advocacy to create success for all people with learning disabilities.

ldaamerica.org

ACKNOWLEDGEMENTS

To God

You're the reason all these awesome people came into my life at just the right miraculous moment and helped me not just survive, but overcome. Thank you for helping me smile through everything. Thank you for loving me and giving me a vision of love and service for my life!

To My Parents

You're the reason I know what true love and laughter are. Thank you for dedicating your lives to me and modeling Christ.

To My Grandparents

Papi and Nani, Pa and Ma, you're the reason I have a solid foundation and a hope-filled future. Thank you for your love and endless support, and for letting me be the JesTer in your life. Thanks, also, to my entire Boll and Mestdagh families!

To So Many Others

There are so many people who have impacted my life and this book. I can't list them all, but here are some:

Dr. Fritz Rector: the reason I am alive.

Dr. Doug Ziegler: the reason I had health enough to fight the big battles.

Dr. Alberto Peña: the reason I have "quality of life."

Dr. Pramod Reddy: the reason I try to practice showing care to the whole person.

All my friends: the reason I always had love and support (and TONS of fun and memories!).

Sarah Kennedy Gilpin: the reason I have a sister who has been there for me.

Grace Fenton: the reason I never lost faith.

Ladi Lettovsky: the reason I can "fall" and get back up in life.

Martina Lettovsky: the reason I'm able to practice "pole, pole" every day.

Steve Tattum: the reason I can read and write; and who was the motivation behind writing this book.

Rosemarie Offenhauer: the reason I started to believe in myself.

Denver Academy and Emily Friends Nightcap: the reason school returned to being a magical world to explore.

Dr. Suzanne Klein: the reason thousands of Michigan kids were impacted by F.A.S.T.

Donna Martin: the reason I regained a vision of myself as confident.

Julie Martin Kelly: the reason I reached the top of my game when it came to learning.

P.J. Vlahantones: the reason I stayed motivated to take care of myself.

Dr. Joseph Healey: the reason I succeeded and crossed the threshold in high school.

University Liggett School: the reason I reached for the next level.

Dr. Nido Qubein: the reason EXCELLENCE will always be my starting point.

Pam Wannamaker, Heather Slocum, Suzanne Hawks, Dr. Craig Curty, Dr. Akir Khan, Brielle Tyree and too many to name at High Point University: the reason I had an extraordinary launch into adulthood.

Mrs. Wierda: the reason I found writer Anita Palmer, who helped me write this book.

Anita Palmer: the reason my story is being told in my own words. I will be forever grateful to my ghostwriter.

ABOUT THE AUTHOR

JT Mestdagh is a young entrepreneur and inspirational speaker based in Grosse Pointe, Michigan. A graduate of High Point University in North Carolina, Mestdagh is also an experienced mountaineer, extreme skier, boater, hunter, car-lover, and adventurer who has made it his life mission to encourage people to untether from natural or self-imposed limitations and live full, passionate lives.

Born with life-threatening VATER/VACTERL syndrome, and extreme dyslexia and short-term memory loss, Mestdagh established the JT Mestdagh Foundation to help bring understanding, joy, and laughter to people with physical and learning disabilities, and to their families, and to encourage them to never, never, never give up.

Follow the **INSPIRATION**

Facebook.com/JTMestdagh   Instagram.com/JT_Mestdagh

Twitter.com/JT_Mestdagh   linkedin.com/in/JTMestdagh

To learn more and to receive updates visit
JTMestdagh.com/book

CPSIA information can be obtained
at www.ICGtesting.com
Printed in the USA
LVHW082232081221
705700LV00011BA/83/J